NOW!⚡

CLASSROOMS

GRADES K–2

LESSONS FOR ENHANCING
TEACHING AND LEARNING
THROUGH TECHNOLOGY

MEG ORMISTON

Beth Hatlen   **Kirstin McGinnis**
Kristy Hopkins   **Lissa Blake**
                          Nicole Ring

Solution Tree | Press

555 North Morton Street
Bloomington, IN 47404
800.733.6786 (toll free) / 812.336.7700
FAX: 812.336.7790

email: info@SolutionTree.com
SolutionTree.com

Visit **go.SolutionTree.com/technology** to download the free reproducibles in this book.

Printed in the United States of America

21 20 19 18 17   1 2 3 4 5

FSC
www.fsc.org
MIX
Paper from
responsible sources
FSC® C011935

Library of Congress Cataloging-in-Publication Data

Names: Ormiston, Meghan J., author.
Title: NOW classrooms, grades K-2 : lessons for enhancing teaching and
   learning through technology / Authors: Meg Ormiston; Beth Hatlen; Kristy
   Hopkins; Kirstin McGinnis; Lissa Blake; Nicole Ring.
Description: Bloomington, IN : Solution Tree Press, [2018] | Series: NOW
   classrooms | Includes bibliographical references and index.
Identifiers: LCCN 2017020335 | ISBN 9781945349386 (perfect bound)
Subjects: LCSH: Education, Primary--Computer-assisted instruction. |
   Educational technology--Study and teaching (Primary) | School improvement programs.
Classification: LCC LB1028.5 .O688 2018 | DDC 371.33--dc23 LC record available at
   https://lccn.loc.gov/2017020335

Solution Tree
Jeffrey C. Jones, CEO
Edmund M. Ackerman, President

Solution Tree Press
President and Publisher: Douglas M. Rife
Editorial Director: Sarah Payne-Mills
Art Director: Rian Anderson
Managing Production Editor: Caroline Cascio
Senior Production Editor: Todd Brakke
Senior Editor: Amy Rubenstein
Copy Editor: Jessi Finn
Proofreader: Elisabeth Abrams
Text and Cover Designer: Rian Anderson
Editorial Assistants: Jessi Finn and Kendra Slayton

To my number-one cheerleader, my mom, Marta Hart;
and to my men at home, Brian, Danny, and Patrick.

—MEG ORMISTON

To my loving family, Brian, Libby, and
Mason; and to my first principal, who
took a chance on me, Fred Haber.

—BETH HATLEN

To my parents, Pete and Kay, who helped
me become the person I am today; and to
my family, Brian, Cailin, and Kylie, for the
support and love you provide every day!

—KRISTY HOPKINS

To my family, colleagues, and friends, who
always support all my crazy adventures!

—KIRSTIN MCGINNIS

To my family, Adam, Lucie, and Emerson—
you are the light of my life!

—LISSA BLAKE

To my wonderful family, Justin, Cameron,
and Logan; and to my parents, who always
supported and pushed me to do my best!

—NICOLE RING

Acknowledgments

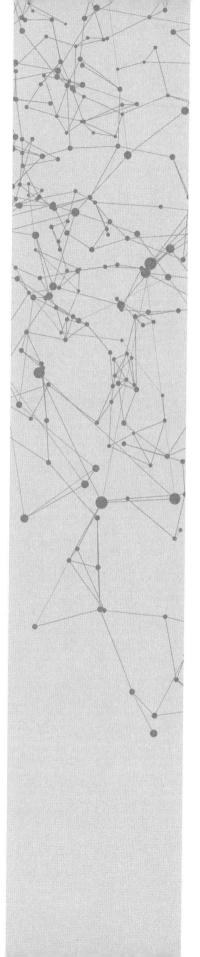

Thank you to all teachers everywhere! I am proud to say I am a teacher, and I believe it is one of the most important professions in the world. Specifically, I want to thank the collaborative writing team that coauthored this series of five books. I have never worked with a more dedicated, fun-loving, collaborative team of lifelong learners. Thanks to the Otus team for your support and to my family for putting up with our writing marathons. I give my deepest thanks to Douglas Rife and the entire team at Solution Tree for helping all of us craft this dream into a reality. Wow!

—Meg Ormiston

Thank you to my students throughout the years who have taught me more about education and learning than any book or other resource could. Thank you to Meg Ormiston for giving me this opportunity to share my experiences with other teachers. Thank you also to my mentors, Robin Bruebach and Matt Rich, who continually push me to grow and evolve in my craft. Thank you to my parents and family who have supported me throughout this life journey.

—Beth Hatlen

Thank you to the teachers I have had throughout my education who have inspired me to become that teacher who tries to understand, guide, and instill curiosity in my students and make learning exciting to them. Thank you to the many administrators who encouraged me to keep learning and growing. You are amazing examples of what teaching should be about. Finally, thank you to all my students, who make it easy to teach from the heart. I would not be who I am without you!

—Kristy Hopkins

Thank you to everyone who supports my dreams, both big and little. Thank you to the colleagues, friends, and mentors who pushed me. Thank you to Greg Michie, who challenged me to think deeper and whose influence consistently grounds me and fuels my fire. And thank you to my students, whom I always keep in my heart and who are the reason I feel passionate about all I do—dream big, my little ones!

—Kirstin McGinnis

Thank you to all the great teachers who helped guide me into the world of education. Thank you for showing me that learning can and should be a fun, exciting adventure. Life is what you make it, so let's make our classrooms so engaging that students would buy tickets to get in!

—Lissa Blake

Thank you to all my past teachers and students who inspired me to become the teacher I am today. Thank you to my administrators, Matt Rich and Robin Bruebach, who continually push me out of my comfort zone and help me grow as a learner and a coach. Thank you to my husband, Justin, who supported me through this journey and always puts our family first. Finally, thank you to my parents, who have been simply amazing!

—Nicole Ring

Solution Tree Press would like to thank the following reviewers:

Danielle Brown
Kindergarten Teacher
Colonel Johnston Elementary School
Fort Huachuca, Arizona

Cori Coburn-Shiflett
Digital Learning Coach
Georgetown Independent School District
Georgetown, Texas

Kandi Marshall
Second-Grade Teacher
Midland Elementary School
Oxford Junction, Iowa

Megan McNinch
K–5 Technology Teacher
Sugar Creek Elementary School
Fort Mill, South Carolina

Amy Musone
Technology Support Teacher
Central York School District
York, Pennsylvania

Visit **go.SolutionTree.com/technology** to download the free reproducibles in this book.

Table of Contents

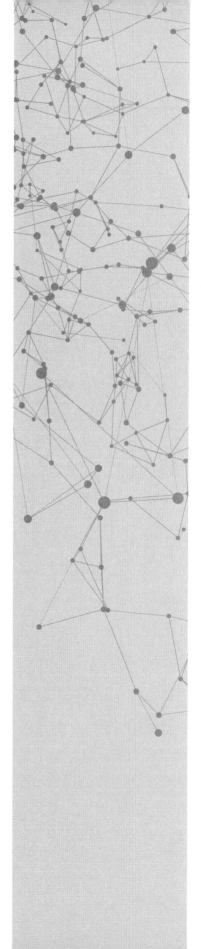

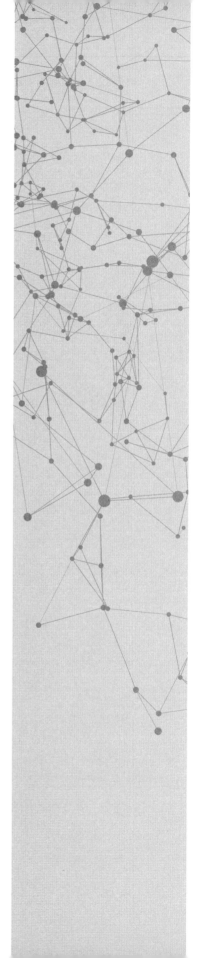

About the Authors

Meg Ormiston, in her role as a consultant, partners with school systems that have committed to 21st century learning experiences for everyone. Meg creates a unique partnership in each district, reflecting the mission, vision, and direction that local leaders identify. Her districtwide projects include guiding teams through the visioning process, designing and delivering professional development, facilitating classroom modeling, developing student leaders in technology, and educating parents.

Meg is a teacher, a keynote speaker, and an author of seven books, including *Creating a Digital-Rich Classroom*, which received an honorable mention in the education category for the 2010 Foreword INDIES Book of the Year Awards. After twelve years teaching and coaching in the classroom, Meg volunteered on her local school board, facilitated grant projects, and continued researching and writing about best practices.

Meg has a master's degree in curriculum and instruction from the National College of Education at National Louis University and travels globally, sharing her passion for real change in the classroom. She lives in the suburbs of Chicago with her husband, Brian; her sons, Danny and Patrick; and her golden retriever puppy, Sonoma.

To learn more about Meg's work, follow @megormi on Twitter.

Beth Hatlen is a kindergarten teacher in a full-day kindergarten program in a 1:1 school district in west suburban Chicago and is currently transitioning to a reading specialist position. Since 2000, Beth has taught preschool and first grade, and she is a certified reading specialist. She has a passion for making learning hands-on, meaningful, and fun while integrating technology into everyday instruction.

Beth was the Downers Grove Elementary Education Association Teacher of the Year in 2012 and a nominee for the Downers Grove Elementary Education Foundation Distinguished Service Award in 2017. She has given presentations on differentiated learning at state and national conferences and on how to integrate technology into the classroom at many district-level in-service days. Beth is a Seesaw ambassador and is active in district and regional collaborations for STEM, language arts, and full-day kindergarten development.

Beth has a bachelor's degree in early childhood education at Elmhurst College and went on to complete two master's degrees in curriculum and instruction and in reading through National Louis University. Beth is a wife to Brian and a mother to a son, a daughter, and a golden retriever.

To learn more about Beth's work, follow @MrsHatlen on Twitter.

Kristy Hopkins is a kindergarten teacher in a 1:1 district in suburban Chicago. She began teaching preschool in an early childhood education program in 2006. Kristy considers herself creative and collaborative and loves to take on new challenges to continue her own learning. She has a passion for helping every student learn in fun, innovative, and developmentally appropriate ways that make every day meaningful.

Kristy is a Seesaw ambassador who holds a special education certificate of approval and an endorsement for teaching

English learners. She was nominated for the 2015 Education Foundation of Downers Grove District 58 Distinguished Service Award and has mentored many new teachers. She has presented at district and school in-service days on how to use technology in the classroom and in social-emotional learning.

Kristy has a bachelor's degree in early childhood education from Illinois State University and a master's degree in curriculum and instruction from National Louis University. Kristy is a wife and a mother to two young girls and loves to spend her free time with her family, go on outdoor adventures, and read anything and everything.

To learn more about Kristy's work, follow @HopkinsKinder on Twitter.

Kirstin McGinnis is a veteran kindergarten teacher in a 1:1 iPad classroom that hosts teachers nationwide for site visits. She feels passionate about providing all students with access to a well-rounded, developmentally appropriate education tailored to each student's needs.

Kirstin is an EdTech consultant and has presented at local, state, and national conferences. She consults for the Technology in Early Childhood Center at Erikson Institute in Chicago and is an elementary education and EdTech blogger at *Hip Hooray in K.*

Kirstin has a master's degree in differentiated instruction from Concordia University Chicago where she is also finishing a second master's degree in leadership. Kirstin loves spending downtime with her husband, sweet baby girl, and dogs, as well as rescuing and fostering dogs, baking, and completing DIY projects.

To learn more about Kirstin's work, follow @kirstinmcginnis on Twitter.

Lissa Blake is an instructional technology integration coach who, for thirteen years, has transformed that role from a computer lab teacher to a true instructional coach supporting K–2 teachers and students. Lissa loves sharing what she has learned by creating exciting presentations that actively engage participants at local conferences and often engage and enlighten all learners.

Lissa is a Seesaw ambassador, Nearpod pioneer, and Google-certified educator and is working to complete her certificate as a Certified Education Technology Leader. She has had the privilege of speaking at local, state, and national conferences.

Lissa received her bachelor's degree in education at Indiana University and earned her master's degree in curriculum and instruction from National Louis University. She currently has a technology specialist endorsement and is pursuing a second master's degree in technology in education. Lissa loves spending all her free time exploring life with her two young girls, husband, and dog.

To learn more about Lissa's work, follow @D60HolmesTech on Twitter.

Nicole Ring serves as an instructional coach in a suburban 1:1 school district. She spent four years teaching fourth grade and seven years teaching first grade. As an instructional coach, Nicole works as a colleague alongside classroom teachers to support student learning and growth. She works with teachers to develop and implement instructional strategies in all content areas while integrating technology in meaningful ways.

Nicole is a Seesaw ambassador and sits on several committees in her district. She was also nominated for the Downers Grove Elementary Education Foundation Distinguished Service Award in 2013. She has presented at local, state, and national conferences.

Nicole completed her bachelor's degree in elementary education and master's degree in curriculum and instruction at North Central College. Nicole maintains a growth mindset, wanting to learn more and more each day, and she loves to spend her free time with her husband and two boys.

To learn more about Nicole's work, follow @NicoleRing58 on Twitter.

To book Meg Ormiston, Beth Hatlen, Kristy Hopkins, Kirstin McGinnis, Lissa Blake, or Nicole Ring for professional development, contact pd@SolutionTree.com.

Introduction: Building the NOW Classroom

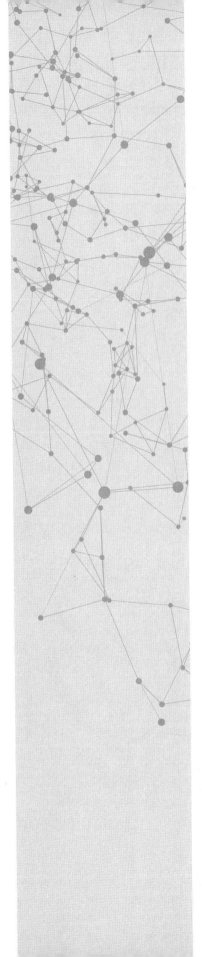

In the perpetually connected 21st century world, teaching and learning lead, but our students need new skills to prepare for their future inside and outside the classroom. We won't find these new skills in dated lesson plans but in adapting our teaching and learning methods to actively engage this connected generation, offering students a voice and choice in how they learn.

As teachers, we want to work in schools filled with magical teacher-student partnership classrooms. In these classrooms, students own their data, and they set individual and group goals based on the projects they are working on. Looking around these classrooms, you see what we call *messy learning* or *organized chaos*. Think of the vibe of a busy coffeehouse, everyone chatting or working independently, depending on each person's goals. Digital devices are everywhere, but so are collaboration and all types of communication as everyone gathers for different goals.

Like in a coffeehouse, when you walk into a magical classroom, you feel the energy as all students are laser focused on their personal learning targets and as they collaborate with each other. The teacher has set high expectations for each student, and he or she continuously monitors data using a variety of technology interfaces. Parents and other professionals are part of the communication loop with access to goal-focused data. We call these magical classrooms *NOW classrooms*. We selected that term because our students deserve to thrive in rich learner-centered classrooms *now*, not in a few months or years. We believe schools are ready to create this type of NOW classroom, typified by technology-supported teaching and learning, and the evidence we've seen bears this belief out. Our goal with this book and this series is to help you create them. We believe teachers and instructional coaches can make this shift even with the youngest learners, and we share that in this K–2 book of the *NOW Classrooms* series.

The central theme of this book and series centers on how teachers can use digital devices to support their primary focus on teaching and learning, offering students a voice and choice in how they learn. We repeat this critical message throughout the book as we concentrate on learning goals rather than on any specific app, website, or device. We filled this book with instructional strategies and lessons that work with technology in the hands of teachers and students. To that end, the lessons in this book use digital devices as educational accelerators, but each lesson specifically ties to an academic outcome. Indeed, this book specifically shows you how academic skills and goals must come before any technology tool, app, or website.

Whether the task at hand uses paper and a pencil or a technology device and digital content, a specific learning goal and purpose should always remain at the core. We don't want to see devices in students' hands when they do low-level learning tasks, or something we call *drill and kill*. Drill and kill misuses technology, and it happens when we focus on the tool or app instead of the learning outcome. As a K–2 teacher or leader, you should concentrate on using technology to facilitate the sort of magical classroom experiences that mark a stark departure from the old days of the computer lab.

Abandoning the Computer Lab Model

Historically, elementary classes isolated technology from instruction. In this old model, the classroom teacher drops off his or her students at an assigned time each week, and someone else teaches technology. My, how things have changed.

Just as all teachers teach reading, classroom teachers now teach technology. The 21st century model of using technology in the classroom starts with the learning goals and then sees if and how technology will enhance the learning experience. The lessons we created for this book will show you ways of using technology to help facilitate learning goals so that you accomplish both academic and technology learning goals at the same time, because teaching time and learning time are precious in the classroom. We want to put technology devices in students' hands not to keep students busy but instead to help them focus on learning outcomes.

You may ask, "What does true technology engagement look like?" This book answers that question by demonstrating the opposite of technology misuse. It features students using technology to create, collaborate, explore, investigate, and share their creations beyond classroom walls. This book structures critical thinking and problem solving into every lesson. It includes meaningful lessons with purposeful technology uses that directly tie into International Society for Technology in Education (ISTE) 2016 Standards for Students. ISTE (2016) education technology experts developed the following seven standards for students:

1. Empowered learner

2. Digital citizen

3. Knowledge constructor

4. Innovative designer

5. Computational thinker

6. Creative communicator

7. Global collaborator

Each chapter in this book references at least one of these standards and connects them to the lesson topics we explore in that chapter. In addition to these ISTE student standards, when we think about engagement and our learning targets, we must think about the important skills of what the Partnership for 21st Century Learning (2015) calls the *four Cs*: (1) communication, (2) collaboration, (3) critical thinking, and (4) creativity. The four Cs, which you can learn more about at www.p21.org, make up a critical part of 21st century learning.

We often think about the future jobs for which we are preparing our students, and, although we don't necessarily yet know what those jobs are, we do know that our students will need the four Cs. To better understand them, take a couple of minutes to reflect on how they break down into the super skills listed in Table I.1.

Table I.1: The Four Cs and Super Skills of the 21st Century

Four Cs	Super Skills
Communication	Sharing thoughts, questions, ideas, and solutions
Collaboration	Working together to reach a goal—putting talent, expertise, and smarts to work
Critical Thinking	Looking at problems in a new way; linking learning across subjects and disciplines
Creativity	Trying new approaches to get things done, which equals innovation and invention

Source: Partnership for 21st Century Learning, n.d.

As educators, we need to create learning opportunities for learners of all ages that emphasize academic content and the super skills inherent in the four Cs. Look for the four Cs throughout the lessons in this book. Our young learners need these skills for their years of schooling ahead and for their future workplace success.

Using This Series

This book is part of the five-book *NOW Classrooms* series, all organized around grade-level-appropriate themes adapted from the 2016 ISTE Standards for Students. The series includes the following five titles.

1. *NOW Classrooms, Grades K–2: Lessons for Enhancing Teaching and Learning Through Technology*

2. *NOW Classrooms, Grades 3–5: Lessons for Enhancing Teaching and Learning Through Technology*

3. *NOW Classrooms, Grades 6–8: Lessons for Enhancing Teaching and Learning Through Technology*

4. *NOW Classrooms, Grades 9–12: Lessons for Enhancing Teaching and Learning Through Technology*

5. *NOW Classrooms, Leader's Guide: Enhancing Teaching and Learning Through Technology*

Instructional coaches might use all five books in the series for project ideas at all grade levels and for leadership strategies. We scaffolded the lessons across the series of books so they all flow together, and we organized all the grade-level books in this series in the same way to make it easy for all readers to see how the ideas link together. We believe this series will save you hours of preparation time.

Using This Book

The primary audience for this book is K–2 classroom teachers with access to technology tools, but instructional coaches and administrators can also use the book's lessons to support the students and teachers they lead. Having access to digital devices in your classroom does not mean you need to have a 1:1 environment in which every student gets a device. We want students to collaborate, communicate, and share with each other, so many of this book's lessons involve grouping students together around a single device. You can also adapt lessons to work in classrooms with limited technology access or those that still use the old computer lab model.

Each of the chapters includes multiple topical sections, each with three lesson levels—(1) *novice*, (2) *operational*, and (3) *wow*, spelling *NOW*. Once we arrived at the three levels, it felt almost like a *Choose Your Own Adventure* book instead of a step-by-step recipe book. Make your lesson selections based on what your students can already do. For example, in chapter 2 of this book, we cover Snapping and Sharing Pictures (page 37). Maybe your students already know how to snap a photo with their device (the novice-level lesson), so you might use the operational lesson, Sequencing Pictures. Students who master the operational lesson can then move on to the wow lesson, Demonstrating Learning Using Pictures, which applies skills in the novice and operational lessons to create new kinds of products.

Each lesson begins with a learning goal, phrased as an *I can* statement, written in student-friendly language. These statements help students understand the learning goal and make the learning experience purposeful. When students more clearly understand what they can do and where they are going, learning happens. This is important because it means that students are taking ownership of their learning. For example, if another teacher visits the classroom, students can articulate the *I can* statement to explain the lesson to the visitor. We then explain to you what students will learn from the lesson, the tools you can use to make it work, and we provide a stepped process you can follow to accomplish the learning goal. All lessons wrap up with two or more subject-area connections with ideas you can use to adapt the lesson to different content areas, like English language arts and mathematics. Along the way we provide teaching and tech tips in this book's scholar's margins to help provide useful insights. Finally, we added discussion questions at the end of each chapter so you can use this book with your team for professional development.

Chapter 1, "Learning Technology Operations and Concepts," is unique to this book and helps you navigate the addition of digital devices and technology to your classroom. K–2 students are just starting out in technology and school, and you should teach them a few lessons before you dive deep into technology projects so that they understand the functionality of the technology they use. We call these technology fundamentals *technology literacy*. Additionally, we cover some essential classroom *learning management system* (LMS) basics to help students understand how to log in and upload content to personal and shared folders.

Chapter 2, "Embracing Creativity," has students work with digital images, capture video, and record audio files as they collaborate on projects. You may or may not enjoy the selfie culture, but K–2 students love taking pictures of themselves, and of course, they love sharing. We embed these 21st century skills into the lessons in this chapter.

Chapter 3, "Communicating and Collaborating," emphasizes communication and collaboration as critical skills for our students. Students will learn 21st century skills that include how to use video to flip learning, how to share appropriately on social media, and how to use live communication tools to connect to local and global audiences.

Chapter 4, "Conducting Research and Curating Information," presents research and information fluency as critical skills for digital learners. Students will learn how to locate information online and check the information for accuracy. Even our youngest learners need these foundational skills.

Chapter 5, "Thinking Critically to Solve Problems," focuses on critical thinking, problem solving, and decision making with regard to selecting and using digital tools. It includes developing students' voice and choice in selecting digital tools to solve problems.

Chapter 6, "Being Responsible Digital Citizens," covers digital citizenship. Teachers always try to protect students physically and emotionally; now this extends to helping students stay safe online. The lessons in this chapter focus on how teachers can help young students have success learning online and stay safe in a digital world. Students will understand why online safety is important and engage in age-appropriate lessons about online stranger danger, cyberbullying, protection of personal information, and intellectual property.

Chapter 7, "Expanding Technology and Coding Concepts," helps you foster 21st century college and career readiness in your students by supporting your youngest learners as they begin understanding the computational thinking concepts that drive how the digital world functions. These lessons introduce students to the basics of computer coding and the language behind their favorite games.

In the appendix, we include an alphabetical list of technology terms and resources. This includes a comprehensive list of apps, websites, and technology tools referenced in this book along with a description of each resource.

Building Background: Know Before You Go

Readers should be aware of a few additional concepts regarding this content before they begin engaging with the lessons and chapters that follow. We want to briefly mention suggestions for the sequence in which readers use the lessons in the book, discuss the concept of learning management systems and common education suites like G Suite for Education that are a critical part of this book's lessons, emphasize the importance of following policies regarding student privacy and Internet use, and discuss how assessment connects with this content.

Sequence of Use

Because every school in every district finds itself in a different place with technology integration, we start this practical book with suggestions for setting up for success. We know some schools ensure they set up devices and install apps before distributing them to classrooms, but we know not every school makes this the case. Chapter 1 is especially for you if your school leaves technology management up to you.

Although we organized this book in an optimal way, we invite you to move among the lessons in whatever sequence you like. Lessons range in difficulty so that you may meet your students at their level. Some second graders will need the very basic lessons, and some kindergarteners will be ready for the advanced lessons. You know your students best, so use our NOW lesson format to fit their needs.

Each of these lessons requires some form of an app or a technology platform to accomplish a learning goal. We offer a variety of suggestions you can deploy with each lesson, but do not limit yourself or your students to our examples. Apps change. They disappear entirely. The best app for a job when we wrote this book may not remain the best one for the job when you read this book. Because of this, we designed each lesson to have adaptability so you can use it with whatever tool best suits your classroom. We don't teach the app; we teach the classroom process.

Learning Management Systems and Education Suites

Just because learning sometimes looks messy, it doesn't mean it lacks structure. Imagine a whole new world without a stack of papers to grade in which the assignments students submit are all organized and recorded in digital folders. Access to technology allows teachers to eliminate the stack of papers and create digital learning experiences that are meaningful and even more powerful to both students and teachers than paper. Schools in the 21st century use many different software programs and web-based applications, or learning management systems to stay organized. Most LMSs have some free features and premium school or district solutions, but regardless of the platform, they operate best when everyone uses the same system so students and parents don't need to learn a different LMS for every class. These systems allow teachers to message students, assign and collect documents, report student progress, and deliver elearning content. Throughout the book, you will notice we provide steps for how you can give digital files to students and then how students return the digital files to you through the classroom LMS.

Common LMSs include the following, but you can find hundreds of others on the market.

- Schoology (www.schoology.com)
- Showbie (www.showbie.com)
- Seesaw (https://web.seesaw.me)
- Canvas (www.canvaslms.com/k-12)
- Edmodo (www.edmodo.com)
- Otus (http://otus.com)
- PowerSchool Learning (www.powerschool.com /solutions/lms)
- Blackboard (www.blackboard.com)
- Moodle (https://moodle.org)
- D2L (www.d2l.com)

One option that needs a little more explanation is Google Classroom (https://classroom.google.com). Google Classroom, which is free to use, is a cross between a document management system and a learning management system. It does not contain all the features of an LMS, but it is a great way to get started with managing a digital classroom.

In addition to an LMS, many school districts use an education productivity suite like Google's G Suite for Education (https://edu.google.com/products/productivity-tools) or Microsoft Office 365 for Education (www.microsoft.com /en-us/education/products/office). We focus on Google's platform because it's the one we are experienced with, but if your school or district uses a different platform, you will find corollaries with them that allow you to adapt our content to your needs.

With G Suite for Education, every user in a district has a unique Gmail login and password to enter their own part of the G Suite, granting them access to the following services.

- Google Docs for word processing
- Google Sheets for spreadsheets
- Google Slides for presentations
- Google Forms to create quizzes and surveys
- Google Drawings to create illustrations
- Google Drive to store and share files

Using these online environments, students and teachers can communicate and keep documents online and available on any device that connects to the Internet. They can keep these documents private or share them with others.

To highlight the value of a product suite such as this, note that our writing team used Google Docs to organize and write this book. Twenty-seven coauthors took part in writing the *NOW Classrooms* series, and none of us can imagine how we could have done this without using a collaborative platform like G Suite. Collaboration, improving work based on formative feedback, and working with digital tools will help even the youngest students prepare for an increasingly technology-driven world so that they can adapt their skill sets to fit newer and better tools as they get older.

Student Privacy and Internet Use

As educators, we make it our goal to prepare even very young students for the world beyond the classroom. For that reason, in many of this book's lessons, you will see students share their work beyond classroom walls. This connection to the outside world is an important one, but before you start tweeting pictures or sharing student work online, make sure you understand your school's and district's policies for sharing information on social media and other public platforms. Talk to your administrator, and ensure that you understand what you can and can't share online. In addition to staying mindful of school and district policy, you should familiarize yourself with the Children's Online Privacy Protection Act of 1998 before you have students publicly share their work.

With this information firmly in hand, you should also make sure that parents or guardians sign release forms for each student that give you permission to post their work online. Even with a signed release form, never share students' full names when you post content on their behalf. Posting work as a class or using private blogs that only parents have access to are also safe and fun ways to introduce students to publicly sharing and receiving feedback on their work. Because Twitter and most other social media platforms require users to be age thirteen or older, if you use one of these platforms to share student work, make sure it is an account that you or the school owns.

Assessment

Formative and summative assessment are integral parts of teaching and give invaluable information on how students are progressing. These assessments also help K–2 teachers to streamline their data and adapt instruction accordingly. We recommend that you use your classroom LMS to house your assessment data and ensure that students and parents have access to it. As students share work, give constructive feedback and record your feedback in your own data files. There are many assessment programs out there that may also be helpful, but because this book features creation-based lessons, we focus this text only on formative assessment options in relation to NOW lessons.

**CONNECT WITH US
ON TWITTER**

Meg Ormiston:
@megormi

Beth Hatlen:
@MrsHatlen

Kristy Hopkins:
@HopkinsKinder

Kirstin McGinnis:
@kirstinmcginnis

Lissa Blake:
@D60HolmesTech

Nicole Ring:
@NicoleRing58

Conclusion

Our team comes from three different school districts in the Chicagoland area. Collectively, we have more than one hundred years of experience in teaching and integrating technology. To better tap this experience while collaborating on this book, we created our own personal learning network (PLN). Many different definitions of a PLN exist, but we like this explanation from Karla Gutierrez (2016):

> Your PLN is where you gather, collect, communicate, create and also share knowledge and experience with a group of connected people, anywhere at any time. It is developed largely through social media, such as Twitter, LinkedIn, Facebook, and blogs, helping us form connections, grow our knowledge base and develop ourselves professionally through continual learning.

Our own PLN served as the glue that kept us connected throughout our work together. You can follow it on Twitter @NowClassrooms or using the #NOWClassrooms hashtag. You can also follow us individually on Twitter by following the accounts listed in the margin. Finally, you can keep up with our work on our blog (http://nowclassrooms.com/blog). We know that technology tools will change after this book goes to press, so we want to share and continue to learn with you on our blog and through social media. Think of our team as your personal professional development network.

This journey is just beginning, and we can't wait to see what your students create, build, and share using digital tools. Communicating beyond the classroom is a theme throughout this series of books, and we will show you why sharing student work creates a broader audience for feedback and how to actually manage this in an elementary classroom. Soon, your students will beg you to tweet a picture of their work and then follow up with you later to find out how many retweets they have. Students will fill their digital portfolio and share their work with parents at home. Collectively, we love the way technology allows families to connect with teaching and learning. We could never go back to teaching in a classroom without digital tools. They help motivate our students to create quality work because more people see their work beyond the classroom.

We look forward to hearing about your students' success!

Learning Technology Operations and Concepts

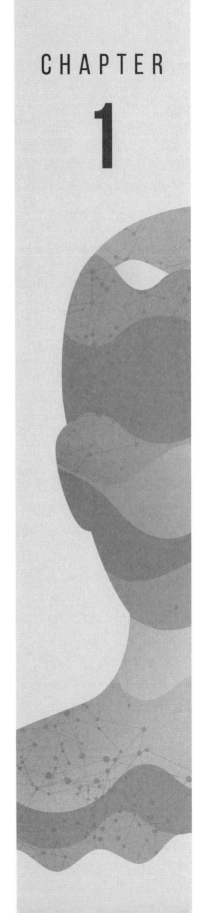

Long before any students use classroom technology, you must establish its purpose and function within your curriculum. Students will use these tools to communicate, collaborate, think critically, and create. These skills—the four Cs—will help them form meaningful connections with what they learn.

With such a powerful purpose, integrating technology tools into your classroom requires a little bit of setup. Some technology departments will lay out all the details for you and provide quality professional development in advance, while others will require you to independently implement the technology deposited into your classroom. We have organized practical ideas to help your implementation succeed, regardless of your circumstances. After you establish your initial organization and follow the short lessons in this chapter, your students will take the reins as they use technology to learn and soar.

In this chapter, we first discuss the introduction of digital devices to your classroom. We then offer some lessons you can use to familiarize students with the basics of operating their device and using common LMS tools like online storage to upload and manage their work. We designed the lessons in this chapter to establish routines and provide your K–2 students with basic technology and platform literacy. We want students to understand basic processes first and learn content more fluidly later.

Introducing Devices to the Classroom

Tablets, computers, interactive whiteboards, and tech toys are cause for much excitement in the elementary classroom and are fabulous tools for education. Knowing that they have their own device gives young students in 1:1 classrooms a great sense of independence and ownership of learning. In a shared technology setting, where you might have carts of laptops or tablets, students will learn the procedures for picking up and storing devices. You can dispense with any fears you may have about your students' readiness to responsibly use these devices. With proper guidance, structure, routines, and maybe some durable cases, you can trust K–2 students to take care of and control their devices.

Your administrator or technology department should have a general plan for device distribution, but you need to discuss with students appropriate use in the classroom so they know your expectations. If you are lucky enough to have one device per student, the device and the carrying case still should have labels. Some districts use student identification numbers or pictures on their device cases. Although the district might have labeled devices through a district inventory process, the system it used may not well-serve young students. In a K–2 classroom, an age-appropriate system using pictures often works best.

In the rest of this section, we cover storing and securing devices, choosing apps for devices, and teaching students to responsibly use their devices.

Storing and Securing Devices

Once you have the devices in your classroom, the question becomes, How will we store them at school for easy access? And, if they go home, What process do we have for that? If the devices remain in the classroom, then charging devices creates a challenge due to the need to plug them all in. One solution is to use portable carts with charging and security

TEACHING TIP

Before you give students devices, plan a process for labeling and distributing the devices. You can use a picture of the student on his or her device, color-coordinated cases, student IDs, and so on. As long as the process enables students to easily find their device in the devices' storage space, any organization system can work.

TECH TIP

Add each student's picture to the lock-screen background on his or her tablet or computer. Students can do this independently by taking a selfie of himself or herself (see chapter 2, page 35, for lessons on taking and using photos). This makes finding their devices easy for all students—non-readers included.

options, but these quickly become expensive. Some other ideas for device storage include charging bins, milk crates, and shelves. You can use Pinterest (www.pinterest.com) as a great source of inspiration for storage ideas if you have not reached a solution. If you need to secure school-owned devices during the day or overnight, have a plan for that too. For example, have a secure location that lets you both charge devices and keep them locked up. Many districts that do not send the devices home have storage carts that, when plugged in, charge student devices.

If students take school-owned devices home, make sure you have a checkout system in place. For example, numbering devices and assigning them to each child often simplify checkout for K–2 students. You can also use a simple pocket chart to organize which school-owned devices go home with each student.

In addition to securing the physical devices, you also need to consider how to secure devices against malicious or inappropriate content. If your classroom uses school-owned devices, your technology should already have uniform security settings the school prefers. For example, one of the great things about using Chromebooks in the classroom is the district typically handles device management. Google has management software it can customize by turning specific features on or off. You just need to make sure you charge the Chromebooks, and then students log in with their school-provided Google accounts.

However, if you must oversee security settings, you should familiarize yourself with the options available to you and consult with your technology department on how to change settings to keep inappropriate content off school-owned devices. If you are in a school in which students bring their own devices (BYOD), consider creating a list of recommended apps and settings that you can share with parents. You should also ensure you're aware of various student-friendly versions of common resources. For example, using Safe YouTube (http://safeyoutube.net) allows you to filter YouTube (www.youtube.com) in a way that will keep inappropriate content away from students. Student-friendly search engines such as KidRex (www.kidrex.org) can also help keep your students safe online.

Choosing Apps

Once you have done what you can to solidify devices' safety features, you need to choose some apps or programs appropriate for student use. Each district handles the app-selection process a bit differently. Sometimes individual teachers choose the apps for students to use, sometimes selections come from grade-level committees, or instructional tech departments might have a hand in this process. To the extent that you have input, select a handful of apps associated with your lesson plans, either district-provided applications or ones we recommend throughout this book. Starting with those few apps, organize apps on the devices to make the optimal impact, and then stick to them throughout the school year. If you are working in a BYOD environment, you can ask the parents to set up the devices with the apps you or your school selected. Regardless, helping K–2 students keep their devices organized means ensuring you or parents nicely arrange apps on the home screen or quick launch bar. On a laptop, using shortcuts on the desktop screen or on the task bar makes frequently used applications easy to access. Students need to see the apps that they should use without feeling overloaded with excess options.

Additionally, when planning which apps and programs to include, always remember content comes first. Ruben Puentedura's (2012) substitution, augmentation, modification, and redefinition (SAMR) model helps teachers design content-based lessons that use technology to enhance those lessons. The SAMR model framework (see figure 1.1) helps teachers talk about the sophistication of technology use in the classroom.

As an example of using this model, students practicing letter formation may visit multiple independent learning centers that you set up around your classroom, such as a sand-tracing center, a pencil-tracing center, a letter-matching center, and a technology center that has a letter-tracing app. The content is learning letters, and the activities allow students to learn letters through a variety of modalities. The SAMR model helps teachers scaffold lessons from simple substitution to redefinition. You can find more information about the SAMR model on our blog (http://nowclassrooms.com/samr-model).

TECH TIP

On Apple devices, you can disable the Safari web browser (www.apple.com/safari) and require students to use only the apps you provide on the devices, such as a student-friendly search engine app.

TECH TIP

Consider using folders to organize apps or tools by topic on a device. In Kirstin's iPad-driven classroom, for example, she has students put often-used apps on the dock at the bottom of the home screen. They organize any additional apps into labeled folders. If your students use Chromebooks, there are no additional apps for you to organize because everything is organized within G Suite for Education as an add on or a browser extension.

Transformation	**Redefinition:** Technology allows for the creation of new tasks, previously inconceivable. For example, create a narrated Google Earth guided tour and share this online.
	Modification: Technology allows for significant task redesign. For example, use Google Earth layers, such as Panoramio and 360Cities, to research locations.
Enhancement	**Augmentation:** Technology acts as a direct tool substitute, with functional improvement. For example, use Google Earth rulers to measure the distance between two places.
	Substitution: Technology acts as a direct tool substitute, with no functional change. For example, use Google Earth instead of an atlas to locate a place.

Source: Adapted from Puentedura, 2014.

Figure 1.1: The SAMR model.

Teaching Device Responsibility

By now, you have done most of the behind-the-scenes setup, and you can start introducing iPads, Chromebooks, laptops, or other tablets to your students. We like to start with a whole-class meeting about responsibility. Chances are most students have played with a smartphone, tablet, or computer and can use their background knowledge to fill out an anchor chart on how to responsibly use the device, like the one in figure 1.2 (page 20).

For K–2 students, use visuals, and make the key points simple—you can modify this example to fit your classroom or add to the chart later. Hang the anchor chart up in a prominent place in your room, and review it daily early on in your implementation. Don't forget to praise those students you see following the chart.

Figure 1.2: Sample anchor chart for using iPads responsibly.

Although we present multiple options in this chapter, each district, school, and classroom tackles device management in a different way, so don't obsess too much about it. Instead, find solutions that will work in *your* classroom for *you*. Students' abilities will change throughout the year, as will your expectations of them.

Learning Basic Operations and Troubleshooting

Students become independent when they work with digital devices as tools and can troubleshoot with peers to become technology literate and technology fluent. The NOW lessons in this section focus on equipping K–2 students with device basics, like learning basic keyboarding and navigation, asking for help to solve problems, and solving problems without help. These lessons require repetition for students to become proficient.

Novice: Using Basic Keyboarding and Touch-Screen Navigation

Learning how to properly use a keyboard, whether with an on-screen or physical keyboard, is important to success with technology, and this lesson provides separate processes for each scenario. This lesson introduces students to the keyboard by having them practice finding keys on a paper keyboard as a whole group, individually, or in learning centers. By practicing on paper, as shown in figure 1.3, students become familiar with the keyboard layout and will have an easy transition to using an actual keyboard.

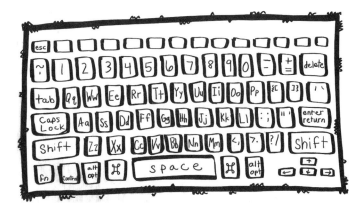

Figure 1.3: Sample keyboard anchor chart.

This lesson also introduces websites that help students with basic keyboarding practice. Some web resources you can use include ABCya keyboarding practice (www.abcya .com/keyboarding_practice.htm), Big Brown Bear keyboarding (www.bigbrownbear.co.uk/keyboard/index.htm), and the TypingClub Chrome extension (search the Google Chrome Web Store at www.google.com/chrome/webstore). Keep practicing this novice lesson with students for two to three weeks.

If students use devices with touch screens (such as tablets), you will also need to teach students how to use the touch feature on these devices. You may have your students use their

Learning goal:
I can use basic keyboarding and touch-screen navigation.

finger or a stylus. For the Using a Touch Screen process, you can install and use any mathematics or literacy app with manipulative tiles, such as ABC Magnetic Alphabet, 10 Frame Fill, Writing Wizard, iWriteWords, Tangram Free, or Schoolkit Math. (Search your device's app store for these apps.)

Process: Using a Keyboard

Use the following five steps to help students become familiar with key locations on a keyboard.

1. With input from students, create a large class keyboard on chart paper.

2. Each day during the classroom's morning meeting, or another selected daily time, help students practice finding letter keys on the paper keyboard by pointing 1–1 (one finger to each letter), matching those keys with corresponding flash cards, or sticking corresponding sticky notes on the chart.

3. During the practice period, give students individual blank keyboard practice papers, like figure 1.4. Continue the practice period at your own discretion based on students' learning and comfort levels when locating letters on the keyboard.

4. Have students play a game of search and find with their individual blank paper keyboards. Hold up a letter or number card and, when students find the letter or number on their paper keyboard, have them color in the key. You can extend this activity by calling out letters they should search for, pointing to letters in sequence, or showing pictures of objects or animals while students find the corresponding letter sound on their paper keyboards. For example, if you hold up a picture of a cat, students should color in the *C* on the paper keyboard.

5. Have students practice their keyboarding individually or in learning centers using the websites we listed for this topic.

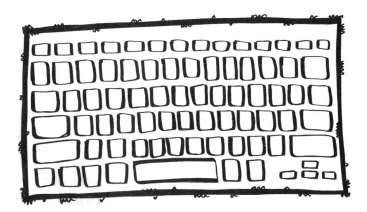

Figure 1.4: Blank keyboard for students.

Process: Using a Touch Screen

Use the following eight steps to introduce students to operating a touch-screen device. (We based these instructions on the ABC Magnetic Alphabet app, but you can substitute your own preferred app that has manipulative tiles.)

1. Select the app you plan to have students use for this lesson, and ensure each student's device has it installed and ready to use.

2. In a small group, gather students with their devices.

3. Discuss with students that when they use their device, their finger becomes a tool. Students must make sure their hands are clean and ready.

4. Model that their finger should not tap the device too hard, but rather should move slowly and steadily. If they press too often or for too long, they could confuse the device.

5. Tell students to locate the app on the device's home screen and tap it once to open it. You can use your own device to model this process.

6. In the app, model for students how to move letters and create words. In the Magic Letters app, for example, drag letter tiles from the bottom of the screen to the middle of the screen. Show them that they can use these letters to spell their name, sight words, or sentences.

Learning goal:
I can discuss technology glitches with peers to solve a problem.

7. Have students drag letter tiles using their finger or a stylus to make their name.

8. When students have finished, give them five minutes to explore other functions of the app as you observe how each student works. For example, most apps in this class have games and other activities to practice with that exist outside this lesson's scope; let the students explore these activities and report back to the class what they discovered.

Connections

You can apply this lesson to different content areas in the following ways.

- **English language arts:** Have students color in their name on their paper keyboards and then have them type their name on a computer or tablet keyboard.

- **Mathematics:** Have students color the numbers 0–9 on their paper keyboards and then have them type numbers in a sequence using the keyboard on their computer or tablet.

Operational: Seeking Help From Peers to Solve a Technology Problem

Students at this age are often just learning that electronic devices don't always work the way they're supposed to, and it's important to arm them with knowledge that can keep the classroom learning experience on track. For this lesson, introduce students to the technology word *glitch*, and instruct them on how to troubleshoot a problem with the help of peers. Some common device glitches include charging problems, a frozen device or app, and password problems. Additionally, working with a peer to problem solve helps students gain collaboration skills, which will transfer into independent troubleshooting and a variety of academic learning activities.

Because the purpose of this lesson is to lay the foundation for independent problem solving when working with digital devices, it helps to introduce students to some common troubleshooting techniques ahead of time. For instance, students should know how to:

- Recognize universal technology symbols and language (camera, trash, share, record, settings, text, close, type, voice, and so on)

- Manually close stuck apps

- Shut down and restart devices when they freeze or another glitch arises

- Plug and unplug devices to charge them

- Respond if an alert pops up (Students should always ask you before pressing anything that unexpectedly appears on their screen.)

With this information, students already have an excellent foundation for working together to solve common problems.

Process: Solving a Technology Problem

Use the following four steps to teach students how to work together to identify and solve basic problems they may encounter with their devices.

1. Create an anchor chart, like figure 1.5 (page 26), to discuss with students a glitch or problem that may come up when using classroom technology.

2. Discuss with the class what students can do to solve the problem.

3. Ask students to work together and use the anchor chart as glitches arise on their devices. If they can solve a problem, have them discuss the problem and how they solved it with the class.

4. When students face a problem they can't solve together, have them discuss it with you, and make it a teachable moment for the class that you can then add to the anchor chart.

Connections

You can apply this lesson to different content areas in the following ways.

- **English language arts:** Have partners clarify and discuss what a glitch is and give personal examples of glitches they have encountered while using different types of technology. Work with their examples to build a new anchor chart that addresses problems they experienced.

- **Mathematics:** Partners work with their device's calculator app to practice doing simple mathematics problems and then pressing the *C* button to clear the previous problem before moving on. Students should talk together and problem solve how to reset the calculator if it does not clear properly or if a glitch appears.

Figure 1.5: Sample anchor chart to help students solve a glitch on a device.

Wow: Solving Technology Problems With Tech-Sperts

In this lesson, students will extend their existing learning by becoming *tech-sperts*—technology experts at a specialized task. Using tech-sperts in the classroom is a management strategy that helps students collaborate to solve technology problems. In this way, students learn to take over responsibility for solving problems so you, as their teacher, can focus on instruction. To that end, you will facilitate a discussion on what it means to become a tech-spert and explain that your classroom will assign student tech-sperts to help peers solve

Learning goal:

I can become a classroom tech-spert at a specific task, and I know who other classroom tech-sperts are that I can talk to so I can problem solve a technology glitch.

problems with specific apps or devices. The purpose of this lesson is for students to independently identify how to solve a problem or when to seek additional help with technology.

Process: Nominating Tech-Sperts

Use the following three steps to guide students through the process of becoming experts in a technological process and then nominate students as tech-sperts for individual tasks.

1. Lead a class discussion on what *expert* means. Then, with your class, define the term *tech-spert* as a technology expert. Explain to students that they will each become a tech-spert with an application, a program, or at taking care of devices.

2. Through observation and notetaking, evaluate students' fluency with using specific applications or device features in your classroom. As you identify individual student strengths, solicit volunteers who can answer questions about specific apps or glitches, and nominate them as tech-sperts for their area of expertise.

3. Create and share a tech-spert anchor chart, like figure 1.6 (page 28), with your class so students know whom to go to when glitches or questions arise. Continue to monitor student abilities throughout the year and update your anchor chart as students gain proficiency in a variety of applications.

Connections

You can apply this lesson to different content areas in the following ways.

- **English language arts:** Have partners work together to discuss advanced features of different apps and websites that you use in the classroom that are related to language instruction. Through classroom discussion, identify which students best understand a given app or website and nominate them as classroom tech-sperts.

- **Mathematics:** Have classroom tech-sperts demonstrate how to use a mathematics app related to classroom instruction. Make them available to other students to answer any questions they have when trying to use the app.

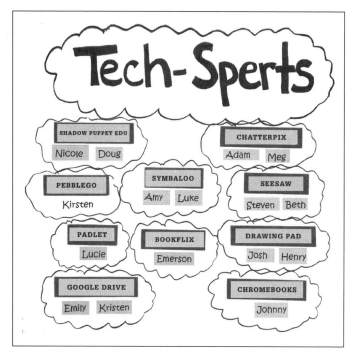

Figure 1.6: Sample anchor chart for identifying tech-sperts.

Introducing LMS Features to Students

An important component of the four Cs, communicating or sharing through technology allows students to share all the wonderful work they do in school (Partnership for 21st Century Learning, 2015). This sharing should include parents so they know about the projects students create and they receive frequent and relevant updates on student work and progress. As we noted in the book introduction, your school or district likely has an LMS in place for you to use for communication and sharing, but if it doesn't, you can set one up for your classroom to facilitate student sharing with both peers and parents.

An LMS plays a key part in classroom communication and sharing student work, but before introducing an LMS to students, you must understand its features and tools and how you can make use of it in your classroom. Once you learn the ins and outs of your classroom LMS, you can easily share it with students and begin using it in the classroom for workflow, digital portfolios, formative assessment, collaborative projects, and connections to home. This NOW lesson set focuses on helping orient students with uploading and sharing content using a classroom LMS.

Novice: Getting Started With an LMS

Whether it is one your school or district provided, or one you set up, the purpose of this lesson is to teach students how to log in to the classroom LMS. This is likely to be new territory for your K–2 students, so it's important that they understand the act of using personal credentials to log into a digital platform. This basic skill will serve them well throughout the year and in future grades as they begin using other apps and services that require logins. As part of this process, you need to make sure your classroom LMS is set up with profiles for each student.

Process: Logging Into an LMS

Use the following three steps to have students log in to the classroom LMS and get familiar with its environment.

1. After setting up a classroom profile in your chosen LMS, ensure each student has a log in they can use, and then create a personal portfolio space for them to upload their work and a shared space where peers can share work with the entire class.

2. Model for students how to log in using the LMS you selected. During LMS setup, many systems create *quick codes* that you can send to your students to make it easier for them to access the LMS.

3. Have students log into the LMS. Look for and provide assistance to any students having trouble.

Learning goal:
I can log in to my classroom LMS.

TEACHING TIP

If you have a combination of students who are new to the LMS and students who are already familiar with it, nominate some of the experienced students as LMS techsperts and have them help students who are struggling.

Connections

You can apply this lesson to different content areas in the following ways.

- **English language arts:** Have students practice newly-learned knowledge about alphanumeric characters and keyboards to enter a quick code or email and log in to their classroom LMS.

- **Mathematics:** Conduct a classroom discussion about the power of numbers to make it simpler to accomplish common tasks on digital devices, like using PINs as quick codes to log into an LMS.

Operational: Uploading Content to an LMS

Learning goal:
I can upload my work to a personal or shared folder on the classroom LMS.

Most LMS platforms provide online storage space for students to upload and share documents. Sometimes this space is something unique to the LMS, while some systems use existing cloud storage platforms like Google Drive. Regardless of which setup your classroom LMS uses, we designed this lesson to help you introduce students to common images and icons associated with uploading their work to the classroom LMS. Students will practice uploading content and understanding the difference between personal and shared spaces and when they can make appropriate uses of each.

Process: Uploading Files to a Personal or Shared Classroom Folder

Use the following five steps to help students look for the share or upload button on the classroom LMS and upload their work to a personal or classroom portfolio space.

1. Familiarize students with what the upload function looks like in your classroom LMS by compiling examples of common uploading and sharing icons like those in figure 1.7.

2. Have students open the classroom LMS on their devices. Explain to them that the LMS can act as a storage space to house and share their work. Explain the difference between personal and shared spaces in the classroom LMS and how to tell the difference between them.

3. Tell students to find and select the option to share or upload a document within the LMS.

4. Help students follow the LMS prompts to select the type of content they want to upload and then select between personal and shared spaces to upload it.

5. Have students practice uploading documents, pictures, and videos from their devices to both personal and shared spaces in the classroom LMS.

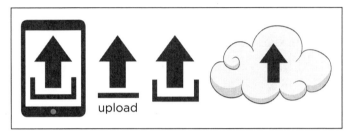

Figure 1.7: Common uploading icons.

Connections

You can apply this lesson to different content areas in the following ways.

- **English language arts:** Set up a private reading space where students can go with a tablet or computer that can record them reading. (You will learn more about completing video- and audio-recording activities in chapter 2.) Have students choose a book at their independent reading level and then record themselves reading the chosen book, saving the video recording to their photo album or desktop. Students then open the classroom LMS and upload the video to their individual folder.

- **Mathematics:** Have students take a picture of a mathematics problem they solved and upload their solution to a shared folder in the classroom LMS. (We offer lessons for instructing students on taking simple photos in chapter 2.) Show students how their work appears in the shared folder and how they can view what their peers uploaded.

Learning goal:

I can use an LMS to access, edit, and update existing content and then save and share it.

 DISCUSSION QUESTIONS

Consider the following questions for personal reflection or in collaborative work with colleagues.

▸ What are some practical and student-centered ways to store and secure your devices within the classroom or school?

▸ How does your district handle making learning apps available on students' devices? What impact do you have in this process?

▸ Can you define the SAMR model? What is an example of a lesson you use in your classroom and how it may differ relative to each level of the SAMR model?

▸ What are some important ways to handle the physical care of classroom devices? What are the most critical items to teach to your students?

Wow: Updating Existing LMS Content

As students become more proficient with using the classroom LMS, you can begin laying the groundwork for them to better utilize other LMS components by having them update existing content. By helping students learn to successfully edit an item they previously uploaded to an LMS, they learn how easy it is to improve the quality of their work through editing. Understanding this process will help both you and your students to better understand the power of a paperless classroom.

Process: Editing an Existing Work

Use the following three steps to have students update an existing product on the classroom LMS.

1. Offer students feedback on work they previously uploaded. If you're not ready to have students update their own work, you can put a work sample you created into a shared classroom folder and tell students how you'd like them to edit it. In either case, have them download the item to their devices.

2. Have students open the content item they downloaded (images, text, and so on) and improve the work based on your feedback or other instruction. For example, students can edit or add to their work using recordings, drawings, or combined images. Whatever level of work they are comfortable with is OK, as long as they are adding to or changing content in some way.

3. Have students save their product under a new name and upload it to their personal folder on the classroom LMS. Learning how to rename files when creating a new product will help them learn to avoid overwriting existing content in a personal or shared folder. Make sure to explain to students why this is important and lend help throughout the process to students who are struggling to use their digital tools.

Connections

You can apply this lesson to different content areas in the following ways.

- **English language arts:** Create a sample text document that contains a simple sentence that includes a spelling error that your students can identify. Place it in a shared LMS folder. Have students download and open the file, locate and fix the error, and then re-upload it to their personal folder on the LMS.

- **Mathematics:** Create a photo or screenshot file with two mathematics problems your students understand. One problem should show a correct solution and one an incorrect solution. Upload it to a shared classroom folder. Have students download and open the file in an image-editing app. Students should draw an *X* on or near the incorrect problem, save the file, and then re-upload it to their personal folder on the LMS.

Conclusion

The goal of using technology in the classroom is to help students communicate, collaborate, and think critically inside and outside the classroom. The lessons and tips in this chapter will prepare your students for successful technology use in your classroom, so that in chapter 2, students are better equipped to use their devices to create and show off all types of digital projects.

▶ How can using a paper keyboard lead to improved keyboarding skills? Why?

▶ Why is it important to nominate classroom tech-sperts, and what strategy will you use to determine who the class tech-sperts will be for a given app or device feature?

▶ Why is it important to seek the advice of peers to solve technology problems?

▶ How will you define a glitch to students, and what will you teach them to do to deal with one?

▶ What are the strengths and weaknesses of the LMS app you use in your classroom? How will you teach your students to take advantage of strengths and work around weaknesses?

Embracing Creativity

In its 2016 Standards for Students, ISTE lists creating *empowered learners* as one of an educator's core jobs in the 21st century classroom. Specifically, "Students leverage technology to take an active role in choosing, achieving and demonstrating competency in their learning goals, informed by the learning sciences" (ISTE, 2016). Elementary classrooms include many ways for students to learn to use technology in a fun, meaningful way and create innovative products. It starts with baby steps, like setting simple goals for students that you can use technology to achieve, and builds on those steps with varying levels of difficulty.

Consider the simple act of taking a picture. Most students enjoy taking pictures of themselves or their friends. In this selfie-filled world, even young students know the value of taking a picture and sharing it with their friends. Even if they're not aware of it, it's about making choices. "Learning that incorporates student choice provides a pathway for students to fully, genuinely invest themselves in quality work that matters. Participating in learning design allows students to make meaning of content on their own terms" (Block, 2014). When students take ownership and make something to call their own, technology becomes much more meaningful to them.

You can introduce technology in the classroom in a fun way by connecting it directly to students; make it about them. We believe that no better way to do this exists than to have them take pictures of themselves and their classmates. Although the baby step of snapping a picture may not immediately appear innovative, it's an easy place to start. Starting small introduces camera tools and different ways to capture and use photos in fun ways. From here, you can layer in complexity that eventually leads to great, student-produced products that show their true creativity.

As students build familiarity with their device's camera and taking photos, teachers can then move on to using videos. This is more complex, but after a bit of practice, even the youngest students can move from one level of learning to the next with their video-creation skills. When you present a lesson that students find meaningful to their learning, they can create video projects that show what they have truly learned and what they understand in an extremely creative and innovative way. Because teachers can conduct quick check-ins with student groups working on a video project, and then pace and restructure lessons according to their learning, video is also a useful formative assessment tool. Likewise, teachers can use video for summative assessment by having student groups plan and shoot a video to show what they learned during a study unit. Finally, students can create a strong school-home connection by sharing videos with parents and other family members.

Introducing audio gives students another wonderful way for them to share their learning and to connect with others. It may feel counterintuitive that we introduce video lessons before lessons on audio, but in our experience, most students already have a solid understanding of basic video components and concepts. It comes naturally to them, whereas working with audio in isolation is often new to them. Using audio without video, however, has unique benefits. For example, teaching English learners to use audio features can help them hear the proper pronunciation of words while allowing all students to self-assess, monitor their own growth as they work, and set goals for future progress. When students replay an audio clip they have a chance to reflect on what they produced, make simple improvements, and then rerecord. Using audio can also help you assess what students have learned because, as you play their recordings, you can specifically identify the skills that each student needs to continue to work on, or decide when it is time to move on to the next set of skills. You can also share audio clips with parents and other experts at the school to show student progress.

In this chapter, we share specific lessons, strategies, and tools for creating learning experiences using pictures, video, and audio on devices.

Snapping and Sharing Pictures

Students learn to communicate and collaborate by snapping and sharing photos and using them, as well as other digital images, to create projects individually and in small groups. Many of your students have experience with taking digital pictures, but after these lessons, they will know how to use those pictures in a learning capacity, share and sequence their work, and demonstrate their learning while engaging in peer feedback with each other.

Novice: Taking Pictures With a Camera App

Students can start using technology in a fun way when they discover how to open and use the camera feature on a device. The goal of this lesson is for students to take pictures to support classroom learning. For example, if students are studying weather, you can have them use the camera app on their devices to snap pictures of the weather each day and use those pictures to talk about concepts like basic cloud formations. For this lesson, you should determine an activity appropriate for using photos based on your classroom learning goals and then teach students how to use the camera app on their personal or school-issued devices. If you need ideas, look at the Connections section for this lesson.

Process: Conducting a Photo Hunt

Use the following six steps to conduct a photo hunt using a mobile or portable device.

1. Teach students how to locate the camera app on their device.

Learning goal:
I can use the camera on my device to take pictures.

TECH TIP

Another popular way to capture images for classroom work is to take screenshots of device display screens. The steps involved in this simple process vary depending on the device. On iOS devices, for example, you can take a screenshot by simultaneously pressing the Home and Power buttons.

2. Take your students on a photo hunt. For example, lead them on a walk around the school, and instruct them to take photos related to a topic you specify.

3. Instruct students to open the camera app on their device when they locate a subject they want to capture.

4. Have students select a subject for their photo and frame how they want to capture it.

5. Have students take each photo by pressing the app's capture photo button. This button may appear on the device's screen, or it may be a physical button on the device.

6. Instruct students to work with a partner to discuss their photos and reflect on what they learned.

Connections

You can apply this lesson to different content areas in the following ways.

- **English language arts:** Ask students to go on a letter hunt around the classroom to find where letters in their name appear in the classroom. Students use their device to take a picture of each letter. This activity helps reinforce uppercase and lowercase letter recognition.

- **Mathematics:** Give students a number-recording sheet, for example, a ten frame or a hundreds chart. Have students use their device to capture images of groups of items or manipulatives that can represent each numeral. This activity helps students see relationships among numbers and count in sequential order.

Operational: Sequencing Pictures

Once students understand how to capture individual photos, you should next have them take multiple photos that fit a theme and learn how to sequence them for a presentation. Sequencing pictures in this way engages students' critical-thinking skills by having them evaluate their photos and delete poor-quality ones.

Learning goal:
I can select pictures from a collection of digital images and sequence them to tell a story.

Selecting photos and arranging them in a meaningful order that tells a story require students to use a photo-collage app or website. Shadow Puppet Edu (http://get-puppet.co), PicCollage (https://pic-collage.com), and PicMonkey (www.picmonkey .com) are all simple tools that allow students to make photo collages. You can find many smartphone, tablet, and PC apps like these. Some apps, like PicCollage, require you to download them to your device. On the other hand, PicMonkey is a web-based app that students can use on any device that has a web browser. This lesson assumes students have already captured multiple pictures on a topic you assigned.

Process: Using an App to Sequence Photos

Use the following four steps to teach students how to judge and sequence their work.

1. Have students use their device's photo album or photo app to look at all the photos they've taken on a topic.

2. Teach students to self-evaluate the quality of their photos and delete off-topic and poor-quality (blurry or dark) photos. Make sure students understand not to permanently delete photos that are not associated with their project. If they do, they may not be able to recover them.

3. Have students open the photo-collage app you chose and import only the photos associated with their project.

4. Have students sequence their imported photos in a way that demonstrates their understanding of the topic. At this stage, teachers may evaluate student work on their devices and provide feedback as necessary.

Connections

You can apply this lesson to different content areas in the following ways.

- **English language arts:** Students can practice their spelling words by walking around the classroom and taking pictures of objects that start with the same letter as the spelling word. Have students insert the

TEACHING TIP

Try introducing students to multiple photo-collage apps and then letting them choose the one they are most comfortable using.

pictures into a photo-collage app and sequence them according to your directions.

- **Mathematics:** Students can create groups of objects with a different number of things in each group. To show their ability to count, they then snap a picture of each grouping and use a photo-collage app to put the pictures in numerical order based on the number of items in each photo.

Wow: Demonstrating Learning Using Pictures

You can teach students who have a strong grasp of how to self-select photos to fit a theme and arrange them in order to show their learning through photographs to a larger audience. In this lesson, students will capture photos, create a collage or similar product through an additional app, and then upload it to an age-appropriate sharing site, which can include a shared classroom LMS folder.

As the teacher, you must determine the most ideal platform for this process and who the audience for this content is. If your classroom LMS doesn't support this process or your goals, you can choose from a variety of sharing platforms, like Seesaw (http://web.seesaw.me), Kidblog (https://kidblog.org), Padlet (https://padlet.com), and Flickr (www.flickr.com), for students to use for this purpose. Make sure you instruct students on how to interact with, share, and view work using the platform you select. Depending on the platform you select, students' sharing audience could include other classmates, other classrooms, parents, or even the public.

Process: Creating and Sharing a Collage

Use the following six steps to have students create a collage and then share it using the platform you select.

1. Have students capture and review photos they have taken on a specified topic.

2. Have students evaluate the quality of their photos and delete off-topic and poor-quality photos.

3. Ask students to open a photo-collage or similar app and import the photos related to their project.

Learning goal:

I can use a camera app's basic functions to take and arrange photos and upload them to a classroom LMS or photo-sharing site to demonstrate my learning.

TEACHING TIP

Remember when sharing student work in public spaces to use a teacher- or school-owned account. As we detailed in the book introduction, students under age thirteen may not create their own social media accounts.

4. Model for students how to use the app to create and save a collage or similar project and then have them try it themselves.

5. Have students access the photo-sharing app or website you selected and upload their final product to it. Most photo-sharing apps can export content to a photo album or cloud storage space like Google Drive.

6. Have students share their project with the target audience you selected. If you are using a public-facing platform, you may need to facilitate this step by posting content on students' behalf.

Connections

You can apply this lesson to different content areas in the following ways.

- **English language arts:** Students can take a picture of something that begins with the letter of the day and upload the picture to a teacher-created Padlet or to another photo-sharing platform. Students review all their words and pictures that begin with that letter and create a digital word wall. You can find a fun example of a digital word wall on the blog page we set up for this book (http://nowclassrooms.com/k-2).

- **Mathematics:** Students can take photos of shapes specific to your grade-level learning target. Students can create a photo collage of shapes and, if they possess the necessary skills, add a name or description of the shape using voice, text, or a drawing. They can then upload them to a teacher-created Padlet or other sharing platform.

Recording and Sharing Videos

As your students master taking photos, they are ready to begin creating videos. This may seem more complex, but because they are growing up in a video-driven world, many of your students will enter the classroom with a surprisingly deep understanding of basic video concepts. With just a little extra instruction and practice, your students can become video stars! By learning how to use digital tools to help them access and understand learning targets, they can create videos with a purpose to communicate their learning with others. So, as you engage with these processes, ensure you make student learning meaningful by giving students a specific, classroom-instruction-related item or task to do when creating and editing their videos. This allows students to reflect upon their accomplishments not only in creating video content, but in how that content demonstrates their learning progress.

Novice: Recording Videos

We designed this lesson to teach students how to use videos to demonstrate their learning and meet their learning objectives. You will give students an assignment based on learning objectives in the classroom that you find appropriate for video recording. When preparing students to record their first video, you should offer them clear directions. Usually, a device's camera app performs both photo and video functions, so in addition to knowing where to locate the app, students need to know how to change this setting. Likewise, most devices store videos and photos in the same place, so you need to make sure students know where to look for their recorded videos and how to differentiate them from any photos they may have taken.

Process: Recording a Basic Video

Use the following five steps to instruct students to record a basic video.

1. Tell students to predetermine what they want to make a video about based on your direction or a personal interest.

2. Have students open their device's camera app and select the video feature.

3. Have students select their subject, point the camera toward it, hold the device steady or place it on a stable surface, and press the record button.

4. When they finish, instruct students to press the record button again to end the recording.

Learning goal:
I can use the camera app on my device to record basic videos.

TEACHING TIP

When having students create videos, offer them guidance as to what makes an appropriate subject. For example, if the lesson warrants it, have students record each other (with permission) or create a reflective selfie-video.

5. Help students locate their recorded video in the device's photo album or photo app and have them view it.

Connections

You can apply this lesson to different content areas in the following ways.

- **English language arts:** Students can collaborate with a partner to create a video of themselves or a friend retelling a favorite story. Use standards you establish in your classroom for speaking and listening to help students determine their goals.

- **Mathematics:** Students can make a design with pattern blocks and narrate a video of the design to say what shapes they used to create new shapes. Students can then collaborate with partners and upload their video to the classroom LMS. You can see students conducting a similar project at our blog (http://nowclassrooms.com/k-2).

Operational: Creating a Video Project

Students who master recording basic video footage can move on to creating a more complex movie with joined video clips. Basic student videos can be very telling and provide you with a genuine performance-based assessment, however, refining videos is an important part of learning with technology. Teaching students how to record and edit a movie that has a clear beginning, middle, and end helps them embrace their full creativity.

Some moviemaking and editing procedures require using more sophisticated tools than a device's camera app. If your students use Apple devices, iMovie is an excellent app for this purpose. We also recommend web-based applications like WeVideo (www.wevideo.com) and Animoto (https://animoto .com), which students can use on any device that has a web browser. These tools include numerous built-in themes and editing features that your students will love exploring as they edit their videos. As students learn, you should model how to create a movie by integrating video clips in a meaningful way.

TECH TIP

All devices with a built-in camera app will have a set location to store video content. Some devices, like Chromebooks, also store images and videos in an online folder such as Google Drive (www.google .com/drive).

Learning goal:

I can create a basic video project using a moviemaking app on my device.

Process: Making a Movie

Use the following six steps to instruct students to create a basic movie.

1. Prompt students to record a video on an assigned topic.

2. Have students open the moviemaking app or website you selected and start a new project on the app.

3. Tell students to select from the available built-in themes for their movie if available.

4. Have students review their videos. Teach them how to separate the footage into shorter clips, deleting clips that they don't find useful (like places where they had to stop and restart a recording because they made a mistake).

5. Have students join the useful video clips together and apply their selected theme to form a more focused and polished movie.

6. As students complete their projects, have them share it with you via the classroom LMS or another suitable platform. Model for them how you access and watch the video.

Connections

You can apply this lesson to different content areas in the following ways.

- **English language arts:** Students can record themselves reading a book. After they finish recording, they save the video in the moviemaking app. Using the editing features in the app, students review and edit out any reading mistakes in their movie before finalizing the product.

- **Mathematics:** Students can record how they solve a mathematics problem. If they make a mistake in solving the problem and need to record a correction, they should edit the mistake out of the final movie.

Wow: Creating a Multimedia Movie

When students feel comfortable recording and assembling short movies, you can teach them how to add more complicated elements to their projects. Basic movies include video and live-recorded audio, which does make them inherently a multimedia medium. The editing tools we introduced in the operational lesson also allow students to add even more advanced elements to their projects. These elements include background music, overlay text, transitions between cuts, and much more. You should help students get to know the options at their disposal—where to find them and how to use them—so they can produce more sophisticated projects. Make sure they know how to export their finished video from the moviemaking app they use so they can access it via their device's photo app or photo album and share it with you or their peers.

Learning goal:
I can create a multimedia movie that includes music, text, pictures, and transitions.

Process: Adding Multimedia Elements to Recorded Video

Use the following four steps to instruct students on how to add multimedia elements, like text and transitions, to their video.

1. Introduce students to the more sophisticated tools included in the moviemaking app you selected.

2. Tell students to choose music, text, pictures, transitions, and any of the app's other special elements that they want to use, and add them to a new or existing movie project. (Options will vary depending on the app they use.)

3. Ask students to save their edited movies, and you should then show them how to export those movies to their device's photo app or photo album.

4. Have students share their completed movie with a partner on their device and then share it with you and others on the classroom LMS.

Connections

You can apply this lesson to different content areas in the following ways.

- **English language arts:** Have students collaborate with peers to record each other demonstrating spatial concepts using positional words like *over and under* or *around and in* and then add audio narration to describe the concepts. You can use similar multimedia movie projects with any literacy concept to help students creatively collaborate and demonstrate their learning.

- **Mathematics:** Have students create a mathematics story problem. For example, have them record a skit in which they act out a simple number sentence using props or people. Students will edit the video using their devices and add multimedia elements such as title, text, credits, transitions, and music.

Recording and Sharing Audio

With the K–2 age group, where students have highly variable reading and fluency skills, teachers often find using audio is an enormous asset. Elementary students who are nonreaders, or nonfluent readers and writers, can still use technology to verbally demonstrate what they know. As with images and video work, this audio can help teachers assess what students have learned. Also, students can use this audio to self-assess and monitor their own growth as they work and set goals for future progress. For example, students can use audio clips to retell a familiar story or demonstrate language fluency. Using the processes in these lessons, you can help students understand that recording their voice allows them to show what they know, explain their thinking, and share their learning with others.

Novice: Recording Audio Messages

Voice recordings have a simple yet strong power to enable students to demonstrate their learning. In this lesson, teachers introduce students to a voice-recording application and instruct them on how to start and stop recording with it. Although recording voices involves a simpler process than, for example, working with video, it is still important to give students a thorough introduction to the concept and tools. Many devices have voice-recording features built in, but many

Learning goal:
I can record my voice to demonstrate what I know.

do not. iPhones, for example, include a Voice Memos app by default, but iPads do not. Fortunately, no matter what device you use, you can locate a simple voice-recording app for it. We recommend Chirbit (www.chirbit.com), QuickVoice (www .nfinityinc.com/quickvoiceip.html), Showbie (www.showbie .com), and Seesaw (http://web.seesaw.me). Whichever app you choose, make sure you feel comfortable enough with it to explain to students how to locate and open it, stop and start recording with it, and access and share recordings.

Process: Recording an Audio Message

Use the following six steps to help students record a simple audio message.

1. Show students how to open the voice-recording app you selected for the class.

2. Help students locate the record button so that they know how to start and stop recording.

3. Tell students to use the record button to record a three-minute (or less) audio piece of themselves answering a question or offering an opinion or commentary. Depending on your students' skill levels, you may need to provide them prompts to help with audio recordings.

4. When they finish, ask students to press the record button again to stop recording.

5. Have students listen to their recording. If it does not satisfy them, they can rerecord it until they feel satisfied.

6. Tell students to save and share their recording with you on the classroom LMS. Saving the recording also enables students to share the recording or reflect on it at a later date.

Connections

You can apply this lesson to different content areas in the following ways.

- **English language arts:** Students can record themselves reading assigned sight words or a passage they select. You or the students' peers can listen for

TEACHING TIP

Audio can help English learners hear proper word pronunciation. You can also have students record audio of themselves saying words in both their native language and English and then share the resulting audio file with their parents so that they can better reinforce language development at home.

correct pronunciations or errors and provide specific, timely feedback.

- **Mathematics:** While recording, students can use their voice to describe coins and coin values. Students record their voices as they sort coins into groups or total amounts. Have peers listen to the recorded audio and guess the coins a student names in the recording.

Operational: Assessing Learning Using Audio

Learning goal:
I can use a voice recording to self-assess my learning.

As students become comfortable recording their voices, they can begin replaying their voice recordings to themselves to self-assess and evaluate their own learning. For example, when students replay what they record, they can check for accuracy and evaluate how well they expressed their ideas. Have them reflect honestly with you about what they like about their work and what they believe they can improve.

Students will no doubt make mistakes as they record, so you should instruct them on how to use the voice-recording app's tools to make simple edits so they can remove any unwanted content. Editing audio is even simpler than editing video, so any students who can complete the operational lesson of the Recording and Sharing Videos topic (page 41) should have no trouble becoming operational at audio editing. In addition to the apps we listed in the novice lesson, students can use Explain Everything (https://explaineverything .com) for this purpose. Explain Everything is a useful app that allows students to record their screen's content as well as their voice in what is often called a *screencast*. For a web-based option, consider using Screencastify (www.screencastify .com), an extension of the Chrome web browser (www.google .com/chrome). Although screencasting does bring video elements back into the process, if you use screencasting tools, keep students focused on their audio.

Process: Recording and Reviewing a Task

Use the following five steps to have students record themselves narrating a process and then check for errors and fix any they find.

1. Give students a related task to complete and then have them open the voice-recording app you selected for the class.

2. Have students record themselves narrating as they complete the task.

3. Ask students to listen to the recording to self-assess if they properly narrated the task.

4. Have students rerecord and edit as necessary to address any mistakes.

5. Tell students to share their finished recording with you on the classroom LMS.

Connections

You can apply this lesson to different content areas in the following ways.

- **English language arts:** Students can take a still photo (see Taking Pictures With a Camera App in this chapter on page 37) and upload the photo to an LMS or workflow app such as Seesaw, Showbie, or Explain Everything. Students record their voice saying something about the picture. For example, students can take a photo of their reading journal and explain their illustrations.

- **Mathematics:** Students can take a picture of a mathematics problem that they solved and upload it to an LMS or workflow app such as Seesaw, Showbie, or Explain Everything. Students use this picture as a foundation to explain their thinking using the audio-recording feature within the app.

Wow: Using Audio to Teach Peers

Students who become proficient with recording and editing audio can use audio recordings along with other media formats as an effective way to teach their peers and share their ideas. Using an LMS or workflow app, you can teach students how to upload an audio sample, combine it with a picture of their work, and share a final product with the audience of their choice. Having students teach each other is a very powerful way for them to learn and is a powerful tool for them to use to provide each other with formative feedback.

TECH TIP

Full-featured portfolio apps, like Seesaw and Showbie, usually allow students to upload products so parents can view their work. This is a great option for creating school-home connections between students and parents. These apps also allow teachers to organize a running portfolio of student work.

Learning goal:

I can make and use an audio recording of my voice to demonstrate what I know and teach my peers and others what I have learned.

TEACHING TIP

If you have a classroom sight-word song or another process for learning sight words, have your students record themselves acting as the teacher by teaching others how sight words sound and how to spell them using your sight-word process.

DISCUSSION QUESTIONS

Consider the following questions for personal reflection or in collaborative work with colleagues.

- What level of understanding did you have with regard to using technology to enhance learning before you read this chapter? What level of understanding do you have now?

- How can you apply essential photo-taking skills in your classroom?

- How might you use digital photos for formative or summative assessment?

- In what way could your students use the moviemaking process to show what they have learned? What is an example of a movie activity you could use in your classroom that uses a concept you already teach?

continued ▶

Process: Teaching a Task to Peers

Use the following four steps to have students record their voice explaining how to complete a task, attach an image to the recording, and share the final product with their peers.

1. Have students create a new project in the workflow app or LMS you selected.

2. Tell students to record themselves explaining how to complete a task and then edit the recording to create a finished product.

3. Ask students to upload an image of their work and attach it to the audio recording to help explain the steps that they took to complete the task.

4. Have students use the app to share the final product with their peers, family, or teacher through the classroom LMS.

Connections

You can apply this lesson to different content areas in the following ways.

- **English language arts:** Have students use their device's camera and a voice-recording app to create a sight-word video that helps other students practice learning a sight word. Students take a picture of the sight word (*cat*, for example). Next, they take a picture of each individual letter (*c-a-t*) to spell out the sight word. Finally, they take a picture of the sight word as a whole (*cat*). Students open a photo-collage app or a moviemaking app, like those mentioned in the Snapping and Sharing Pictures (page 37) and Recording and Sharing Videos (page 41) lessons. Students drop in the images they took in the correct order to spell the word and then state the word. They record their voice spelling the sight word. Recoding in this way helps English learners hear and isolate sounds and empowers peers to teach each other foundational skills.

- **Mathematics:** Give students a mathematics problem related to a current classroom topic. Have them solve it on pencil and paper, taking a still photograph of the problem and their solutions.

Students should import their photos into a workflow app or LMS such as Showbie or Seesaw and record audio describing how they answered the problem. Have students share the final product with a partner before submitting it through the classroom LMS.

Conclusion

Teaching students how to integrate learning with the technology at their disposal presents a critical foundation in their development as learners. The very simple processes of snapping pictures, recording videos, and recording audio have far-reaching applications in learning. This chapter helped establish a connection between the basic learning K–2 students embark on during these formative years and the technology principles and concepts that will stay with them for a lifetime. In the next chapter, we go even deeper into the sharing aspects of classroom work to illustrate the importance of collaboration in developing 21st century learners.

▸ How could you use video to assess your students' knowledge level about a classroom topic?

▸ In what way could you use audio lessons to engage English learners or those who have speech challenges?

▸ How could you share with parents examples of their child's voice recordings?

▸ What is an example of a learning target you teach in your classroom for which an audio-recording activity would enrich student learning and understanding?

▸ How could you use the Using Audio to Teach Peers lesson process as a formative assessment experience for students?

▸ Now that you have familiarity with working with pictures, video, and audio, how will you encourage students to choose the best media to showcase their learning?

Communicating and Collaborating

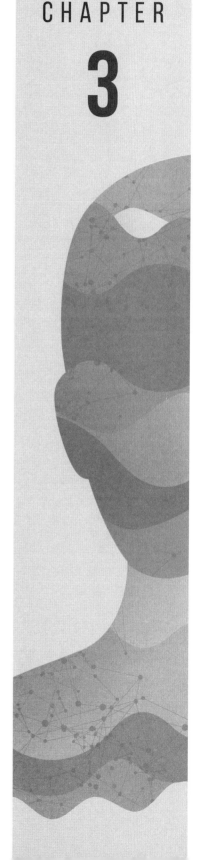

Now that students can create imaginative products, it is time for them to share what they make with an authentic or global audience. In its 2016 Standards for Students, ISTE desires for students to become *creative communicators* and *global collaborators*. In the book *Engaged, Connected, Empowered: Teaching and Learning in the 21st Century*, Ben Curran and Neil Wetherbee (2014) state, "With just a small amount of teaching, students can build collaborative projects and reports with students on the other side of the globe" (p. 33). Now is the time to help students share and collaborate in a kind, meaningful, and safe way.

The lessons in chapter 2 include instructions for having students share their work with each other, either directly or via classroom LMS. That was only the first step. This chapter extends this important skill set by demonstrating how to successfully and safely use instructional videos in the classroom; gain a larger, more diverse audience through social media; and use online collaborative tools to make live connections with an audience. When we see teachers and students learn how to properly share content, and how their global audience takes note, it's amazing how students' interest and motivation soar. Here is how you can get started.

Using Video to Flip Learning

As part of the YouTube generation, our students frequently access online video to learn a variety of things related to their interests. As teachers, we can capitalize on this innate skill to help students use video for lifelong learning. Using videos in your classroom goes beyond watching YouTube. When teachers use technology to enhance classroom learning, it reaps hands-on and interactive benefits. Teachers and students alike can use flipped learning to empower themselves to create videos that help others in the classroom and around the world. *Flipped learning* is an instructional strategy that delivers individual instruction rather than group instruction; learners typically view the video content first, before instruction, and then use classroom activities to demonstrate their learning (the flip).

In their book *Flipped Learning: Gateway to Student Engagement*, Jonathan Bergmann and Aaron Sams (2014) write, "In flipped learning, the direct instruction is delivered individually, usually—though not exclusively—through teacher-created videos" (p. 6). Videos can truly empower students, teach independent learning, and deepen understanding in a significant way. When students watch flipped videos before a lesson, it allows the lesson to activate their prior knowledge and develop deeper learning connections within the classroom. To that end, you can apply these lessons to help students effectively use and create flipped videos.

Novice: Learning From Flipped Video Lessons

We designed this lesson to instruct you on how to facilitate a flipped-learning video lesson for your students to watch. Choose a topic related to your curriculum, and find or record a video of a lesson, an activity, or learning center directions for that topic. Your classroom LMS may offer tools for you to use to do this, but if not, you can use one of the video apps we introduce in Recording and Sharing Videos in chapter 2 (page 41), such as Showbie or Seesaw. If you're starting a unit on oceans, for example, record yourself reading a nonfiction book about the ocean for students to watch in advance of classroom activities that will further develop their new learning.

Learning goal:
I can independently view a flipped-learning video my teacher provides and respond to it.

Process: Taking In a Video

Use the following five steps to share a video with students and have them discuss what they learned from it.

1. Create and upload or find an appropriate video related to a desired curriculum objective. (We offer some ideas for videos to create in the following Connections section.)

2. Share a link to the video with students using the sharing platform you selected.

3. Have students watch the video to complete an activity or understand a lesson. Ideally, students should watch the video at home, outside the classroom. If this isn't feasible—for example, if you have students without Internet access—you can make the videos part of a classroom center for students to complete before the lesson.

4. Have students work in small groups to discuss what they learned from the video. If your students have the necessary writing skills, have them write down three main points that they learned and use them in their discussion.

5. After students complete their group discussions, gather the full class together. Use chart paper to make an anchor chart of all your students' observations from the flipped video. Hang this chart up in your classroom and refer to it throughout your unit, continuing to add observations as students progress.

Connections

You can apply this lesson to different content areas in the following ways.

- **Science:** Make a video of yourself reading a nonfiction science story for a learning center activity. At the end of the story, record yourself asking comprehension questions. When you have completed the recording, save the video, and share it with students via a QR code (see figure 3.1, page 56), an email, or the classroom LMS. Have student partners work together to answer the questions digitally or on a piece of paper.

- **Mathematics:** Choose a mathematics game that supports a concept students are learning, such as Who Has More?, to play in a learning center. In the Who Has More? activity, each player gets half a deck of cards (use just the numbered cards). The partners flip a card down from the top of their deck at the same time. The partner that has the higher-value card wins and takes both cards. Create a flipped-learning video to show them how to play this game. Students watch the video and then play the game on their own in an independent learning center. You can find a similar activity at work at our blog (http://nowclassrooms.com/k-2).

Figure 3.1: Sample learning center activity using QR codes.

Operational: Creating a Flipped Video Lesson

As students become comfortable with the concept of flipped videos you create for them to view and discuss, you can further engage them by having students record their own videos that align with the curriculum and its learning targets. This

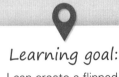

Learning goal:
I can create a flipped-learning video for my teacher.

allows them to communicate their knowledge in a way they can show to others.

For this lesson, make sure you select a moviemaking app for them to use (like Educreations, iMovie, or WeVideo), and let them know which platform you want them to use to share their videos with you (for example, Seesaw, Showbie, or other classroom LMS). Students who are not at the operational level for creating videos can use their device's camera app to record a simpler video. Because this is a new and more advanced activity for students, you must review their videos and offer further instruction on concepts they may not understand yet or feedback on how to improve their videos.

Process: Creating a Flipped Video

Use the following four steps to have students create their own flipped video lesson.

1. Tell students or student groups to pick a moviemaking app they can use to complete a flipped-learning video on a topic you assign.

2. Have students use the app to create a flipped-learning video that describes how to complete a task, lesson, or activity. Students working at the operational level for making movies should challenge themselves by carefully reviewing their recordings and using editing skills to refine their flipped-learning videos.

3. Have students upload their completed video to the sharing platform you specify.

4. Share the videos you approve with the class to help others understand a learning target or to teach others about a new idea or concept.

Connections

You can apply this lesson to different content areas in the following ways.

- **English language arts:** Students can each collaborate with a peer to create a video on a literacy concept they learn. For example, students can create a video that demonstrates their understanding of the differences between fiction and nonfiction texts.

TEACHING TIP

Share a flipped video with parents as a way for them to reinforce student learning at home and to enhance the school-home connection. To enhance their own learning, English language learners can create a translated version of the flipped video that their parents will understand in their home language.

Students can use a variety of images in the video to visually showcase the differences, and then they can record themselves explaining these concepts to their peers using key academic vocabulary.

- **Mathematics:** Students can create a video of themselves solving a mathematics problem. They record how they solved the problem and explain it using a moviemaking app. This helps them better understand the process they used to solve the problem.

Wow: Sharing a Flipped Video Lesson With Peers

Learning goal:

I can share my flipped-learning video with my class.

When students have confidence in their ability to create flipped-learning videos, they can share videos with the class to help others better understand a concept. Having students learn from videos their peers create and share keeps them engaged and further motivates them to learn. In this lesson, students who have a strong grasp of how to create flipped videos should share their videos with classmates using the same moviemaking apps and sharing platforms employed in the operational lesson for this topic.

Process: Sharing a Flipped Video

Use the following four steps to instruct students on how to share a flipped video with their class.

1. Have students create their own example of a flipped-learning video, one based on current learning targets, for other students to use to learn at home or in independent learning centers.

2. Have students upload their finished work to the classroom LMS or another sharing platform you selected. To ensure accuracy, teachers should always preview the videos students create to ensure they are appropriately modeling the learning skill.

3. Ask student peers to view the shared videos and use them to enhance their own learning.

4. Create a folder in your LMS where students can easily access all flipped videos on a specific topic.

Show students how to keep these shared folders organized and use them for reference whenever they need a refresher for a given learning topic.

Connections

You can apply this lesson to different content areas in the following ways.

- **English language arts:** Use an app such as ABC Magnetic Alphabet (search your device's app store) to construct a class make-a-word template, like figure 3.2 (page 60). Have students working on, for example, the short *a* vowel family, use the template on their device to make words in the *-at* word family. Students record a flipped video of themselves sounding out and creating *-at* words using the letters at the bottom of their device screen by moving the letters into place. They can upload their video to the classroom LMS so other students can view it. Videos like this can help struggling readers become more confident in building short vowel words. Additionally, you can use this flipped video for formative assessment by evaluating students' short vowel skills.

- **Mathematics:** Have students use a moviemaking app to create a flipped video to teach other students about a mathematics strategy they have learned. For example, if students are learning about subtraction, they can set up their device and some manipulatives to demonstrate how to subtract. They can take a still photo of three blocks, then one of a person taking away two blocks, then a final picture with one remaining block. They may record themselves saying, "I have three blocks. If I take two blocks away, then I only have one left. That's how you subtract." Students can share their videos with peers to assist each other's learning and with you for assessment purposes.

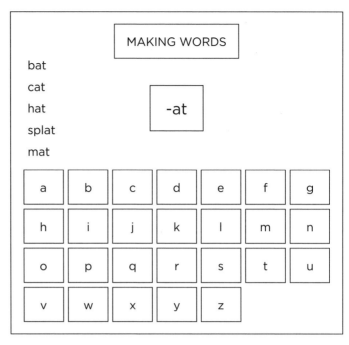

Figure 3.2: Sample make-a-word template.

Sharing With Social Media

You can give students the opportunity to create content for a larger audience than just their classroom peers by having them share their work on social media platforms. With a larger audience, students learn the importance of writing or creating a product worth sharing and how the act of sharing allows them to connect and communicate with family, peers from other classrooms or localities, and even the global community. When students open their eyes to other classrooms outside their own, engagement heightens, and excitement to share becomes real. Allowing for authentic audiences larger than their classroom makes students inclined to improve the quality of their work and gain a broader global perspective (Graham, n.d.).

You have multiple social media platforms at your disposal for connecting with different audiences and classrooms. Some, like those we cover in the Establishing Live Local and Global Connections section, involve live, synchronous connections. The lessons in this section focus specifically on social media tools and platforms and ways to establish connections with other teachers and classrooms.

As we note in the book introduction, most social media platforms have age restrictions that rule out students in the K–2 age group from creating their own accounts. This is for their protection. When we talk about posting content to social media websites in this book, we refer to you, the teacher, posting content using a school account or an account you create for your classroom. Before doing this, check with your administrator to make sure you understand any school or district restrictions for using social media that affect your options.

Whatever platform you use, it is imperative to protect your students by maintaining oversight of who interacts with your social media posts and what your students see. Twitter (https://twitter.com), public-facing blogs, and other platforms do open doors to the darker side of social media, including cyberbullying and harassment, topics we cover in chapter 6. Social media can function as a wonderful platform for engaging students with a global audience, but tread responsibly!

Novice: Creating and Sharing in a Digital Community

The purpose of this lesson is to teach students how to create a piece of work they can share in their own classroom community and with their families. By using an online journal or blog, students will share their creations with others and learn the importance of appropriate and meaningful feedback. When it comes to journaling and blogging, K–2 students' skills vary. Work with them to make them feel comfortable expressing themselves at their skill level.

Some platforms that provide online journaling or blogging features include Seesaw (https://web.seesaw.me), Padlet (https://padlet.com), and Kidblog (https://kidblog.org). As their teacher, you should model ways in which students' peers can comment and collaborate on their work. To this end, conduct a short lesson on what it means to leave an appropriate comment on other students' work. You may find it helpful to leave an anchor chart in the room on positively or helpfully commenting on others' work.

Learning goal:
I can use an online journal or blog to share my learning with my classroom community and my family.

⚡ **TECH TIP**

Most content-sharing platforms allow you to configure how comments publish. You can typically find settings that allow only the teacher to see posted comments (until he or she approves them), while other settings allow students to post comments in real time. Seesaw, for example, allows teachers to choose who can view or comment on student work.

Process: Writing an Online Journal

Use the following four steps to help students post content to a platform where they can share their work.

1. Have students write, draw, or take a photo of their work. Students may also create a product directly on their digital device.

2. Model for students how to upload their work to the online-journaling platform you selected. We suggest Seesaw as it will connect to your students' portfolios and provide school-home connections.

3. Model appropriate and meaningful ways to provide feedback before allowing students to digitally comment on peers' work as a group. Comments on student work can be as simple as a thumbs-up emoji, or as advanced as, "I liked reading your writing about bears. I learned there are many types of bears. What is your favorite bear?"

4. If students are ready, instruct them on how they can view, comment on, and collaborate on each other's work using the platform's tool set.

Connections

You can apply this lesson to different content areas in the following ways.

- **English language arts:** Have students describe a memorable experience that also demonstrates recent language concepts you introduced. Students should describe the experience using an online journal that allows their classmates to view and provide feedback on the work. We include a sample project on our website similar to this (http://nowclassrooms.com/k-2).

- **Mathematics:** Have students create objects out of tangram manipulatives and take a photo. For example, a student could make a sun out of a hexagon tangram and assorted triangles. Students then post their photos to the classroom blog or online journal. Have them comment on the pictures as to what shapes they see. Older students in this grade band may write subtraction or addition story problems and have peers comment with their answers or strategies.

Operational: Connecting Classrooms Through a Digital Community

Once students comfortably share and collaborate within their own classroom community, they can begin collaborating with other classrooms through public blogging platforms. You can extend the reach of several student-friendly blogging platforms by making them accessible to other classrooms using features built into Seesaw, Kidblog, or Edmodo (www .edmodo.com). Introducing this process may require you to do some preliminary homework of your own to familiarize yourself with the sharing options for your classroom blog and find other classrooms to connect with. You can connect with classrooms in the same building or district or with the classrooms of other teachers you've connected with online through a PLN.

Learning goal:
I can use blogging tools to connect and collaborate with another classroom.

This cross-classroom collaboration can help students discover new ways to understand and observe a topic. Additionally, teachers have unique and individual strategies in teaching content, so opening your students to multiple teachers who are teaching the same topic gives them multiple ways to understand the topic. When choosing classrooms to connect with, you may want to consider classrooms that are focusing on the same learning targets. This allows students to collaborate and compare observations on a topic. For this process, model for your students appropriate and meaningful ways to comment on blog posts from the other classroom.

Process: Creating a Cross-Classroom Blog

Use the following six steps to set up a classroom blog and have students contribute to it.

1. Choose a blogging platform, and set up a classroom account to create a blog for your students.

2. Connect your classroom blog with another classroom teacher, either locally or globally. You may find it simpler to start by connecting with another teacher in your own school or district. If necessary, use a PLN to find a teacher to connect with. Twitter

can also act as a great resource for connecting with teachers in other classrooms.

3. Establish communication with the other teacher prior to allowing student peers to view and collaborate on each other's work. Work together to establish your goals for this collaboration and a time frame for when each classroom will contribute work to the blog.

4. Have students use a photo on the blog to prompt comments or questions on daily class activities and learning targets. For example, a student may post the morning message with a question that other students can answer.

5. Ask students to review blog posts from the other classroom. Model appropriate and meaningful ways to provide feedback. For example, you may want to model writing complete thoughts in response to the other classroom's posts. Where in-classroom comments may be less formal, cross-classroom commenting should be formal and well written, so it's helpful to teach students some basic editing skills as part of this process.

6. Allow students who show understanding of proper feedback to comment and collaborate on student work between the classrooms. This allows students to use a genuine learning experience to gain more understanding and acceptance of cultures and children who differ from themselves.

Connections

You can apply this lesson to different content areas in the following ways.

- **English language arts:** Use blogging in association with any literacy activity. For example, if you're working with students on the concept of character traits, at the conclusion of the book activities, use a blog to connect to another classroom that also read the same book. One teacher should select groups of students to blog about a certain character in the book and describe his or her traits. The other teacher should have his or her students comment on which character is being described, adding any additional comments about the character they might have. The other classroom then will do the same activity for another character in the book. Teachers should monitor student comments and conversations to ensure they are accurate and appropriate for the given topic.

- **Social studies:** During a unit exploring communities, connect with a teacher at another school in a different community. (Try using a PLN.) That teacher should have his or her students collect a picture of something important within the community they live, and your students will do the same. Students should post their pictures to their blog and then compare them to the pictures from the other classroom. Students should comment about how the picture is similar to or different from the community in which they live. Because this connection may involve using community landmarks, it's particularly important not to disclose names, addresses, or locations specific to where your students specifically live.

Wow: Connecting With an Authentic Audience Using Social Media

Students ready to extend their sharing and collaboration skills can connect with an authentic audience through social media. This acts as a powerful way to share, collaborate, and learn because students receive formative feedback as well as have pride in sharing final products. For this process, you will create a classroom account using your preferred social media source, such as Twitter (https://twitter.com), Instagram (www.instagram.com), or Remind (www.remind.com).

Because most social media platforms require users to be age thirteen or older, not only must you take great care to protect and abide by the platform's age requirements, you should check with a principal or administrator in advance of setting up a classroom account. You should also send home a permission slip that allows parents to opt out of allowing you to post photos of their child or their child's work to an open social

Learning goal:
I can communicate on social media with an authentic global audience.

TECH TIP

Teachers can have multiple accounts on one social media platform and switch between a classroom account, a professional account (such as a PLN), and a personal account as needed.

media platform. Some districts require you to ask specific questions such as, "May we publicly use your child's picture or work?"

Never forget that keeping students safe is a teacher's number-one job. *Never* say a student's name, age, or location on your public social media page. All social media sites have restrictions you can set regarding who can view information. Check the settings of your desired social media platform for more information.

After you navigate these hurdles, you should model for students how to upload photos, comment, and ask questions related to learning topics. Students will then learn how to create meaningful posts and comments on behalf of the classroom. For this process, you will finalize and publish the posts that students formulate on an account that you or the school owns.

Process: Adding Posts to a Classroom Social Media Account

Use the following five steps to set up a classroom social media account and enlist student contributions.

1. Create a social media account for the classroom on the platform you choose.

2. Model for students how to upload a photo or write a comment or question related to daily class activities and learning targets.

3. Upload a photo or comment to the classroom social media account.

4. Model appropriate and meaningful ways to provide feedback on a post like yours before allowing students to create classroom posts with your supervision and approval.

5. Make sure you review and approve students' posts. You should do the actual posting to the social media account from your own device.

Connections

You can apply this lesson to different content areas in the following ways.

TECH TIP

Although social media platforms like Twitter have age requirements, students of all ages can share work through a private, secure LMS platform like Seesaw or Showbie.

- **English language arts:** During the morning meeting, select a student to practice his or her speaking and listening skills by acting as the classroom's social media master. This could be a position that you switch each day or each week so long as all students have the opportunity sometime during the year. As you discuss with students what the school day will entail, develop a question or comment as a class for the social media master to share, such as, "How do penguins keep their eggs warm?" The social media master uses your class social media account to share the class's question or comment on the day. You could also have your social media master provide a recap of the school day. Having outsiders interact with your classroom by answering the question or replying to the daily update gives authentic learning opportunities to students as well as provides them with opportunities to extend their learning.

- **Mathematics:** Once a month, generate a report from the class Twitter account using the Twitter Analytics page (https://analytics.twitter.com). Once you log into your account, you will see detailed reports on each tweet, including the number of likes, retweets, and views it received. Have students use calculator apps on their devices to add them all up. You can make this an ongoing exercise, by having students compare and contrast Twitter activity from month to month.

> **TEACHING TIP**
>
> When you set up a private social media account, make sure to invite students' parents to follow it, which grants them instant access to what happens throughout the day within the classroom.

Establishing Live Local and Global Connections

In the Sharing With Social Media section (page 60), we introduced the concept of using different social media platforms to share and receive feedback. This section takes that process to the next level by focusing on how you can use live, synchronous online collaboration to promote and motivate students to create high-quality products. As in the previous section, knowing how to offer respectful feedback and collaboration is a crucial component of sharing work. However, live communication requires even more guidance from teachers. All teachers should consistently educate students, no matter their age, on how to respond to their peers in meaningful, productive ways. We suggest you review some Kagan Cooperative Learning Structures as outlined by Gavin Clowes (2011) which we believe are beneficial for students. These are strategies that focus on teambuilding, social and communication skills, knowledge building, procedural learning, processing and thinking skills, and presenting information. It is important to begin by giving students meaningful feedback through live social interactions as a way of modeling appropriate behaviors before allowing them to connect with each other online.

Through thoughtful collaboration at both local and global levels, peer editing can become a powerful tool to help students create their best work.

Novice: Giving Live Feedback to Other Students

Meaningful feedback helps students learn in a powerful way. Much of this book's discussion of feedback focuses on students providing oral and written feedback on their peers' work. For this lesson, you should focus on modeling how students can provide appropriate and meaningful oral feedback in real time to their peers as preparation for making real-time connections between classrooms. Create an anchor chart with sentence starters to help model constructive feedback. Or, discuss some ways that you can respond to commentary that is disagreeable. Once students properly understand these conventions, you should encourage them to independently comment and collaborate on projects.

Process: Giving Oral Feedback

Use the following four steps to model live feedback and collaboration for students.

1. With the whole class, create an anchor chart titled, Colorful Comments. Brainstorm positive comments and feedback that students can leave on other students' work. Some examples include:

   - "I like how you . . ."

   - "Can you tell me more about . . . ?"

Learning goal:

I can participate in an activity that connects with my classroom community and give or receive live feedback to or from others.

- "Why do you think . . . ?"
- "This tells me . . ."

Adding kid-friendly language and comments will help empower your students to provide formative feedback to peers and develop confidence in sharing work.

2. Have students write, draw, or take a photo of non-digital work, anything written or drawn, and post it to the class LMS.

3. Call the whole group back together. Refer to the anchor chart and model an appropriate way to provide feedback on each new piece of posted work. Then, release students to comment on their peers' work.

4. Instruct students to work in small groups or individually and practice commenting on others' work.

Connections

You can apply this lesson to different content areas in the following ways.

- **English language arts:** Ask students to take a picture of a character from a book using their classroom device; upload it to an app such as ChatterPix Kids (http://bit.ly/2u4arGv), Blabberize (http://blabberize.com), or Shadow Puppet Edu (http://get-puppet.co); and retell the book's story from that character's point of view. Students save their work and then upload it to a sharing platform. Ask the class to give appropriate and specific oral feedback about the work the students shared.

- **Mathematics:** Have students take photos of manipulatives to demonstrate grade-level addition. For example, students may take a picture of three red blocks and two green blocks and then edit the picture to draw or write the number sentence $3 + 2 = 5$. Then they can use their device to record a creative number story as pictures or a video. Students can save the pictures or video and then upload them to the classroom LMS. Encourage peers to review and offer oral comments on the number story.

TEACHING TIP

Ensure that students publish an item that they have confidence in and feel comfortable sharing. Talk with them about *wow* work, meaning their best work.

Learning goal:

I can participate in a classroom activity that connects outside my classroom.

Operational: Using Technology to Connect Outside the Classroom

Connecting with classrooms through technology provides a unique way to learn about the world. Some useful platforms for this lesson include Skype (www.skype.com/en), Google Hangouts (https://hangouts.google.com), and FaceTime (http://apple.co/2osx0ld). For this lesson process, we describe using Google Hangouts video chat to collaborate with another classroom in the same building, but you can adapt the steps to whatever live communications platform works best for you and your partner teacher. Work with the other teacher to identify a topic that aligns with both classrooms' curricula. Connected classrooms will learn how to effectively have meaningful conversations online to enhance their learning on a specific topic.

Process: Conducting a Video Chat

Use the following six steps to conduct a video chat between two classrooms.

1. Work with another teacher in your building to establish the tools and learning goals for a video call. Set a time for it to occur.

2. Use your selected communications platform to connect with your partner teacher by exchanging platform contact information and then connecting for a chat (without your students present).

3. Work with your partner teacher to find a common theme in the curricula that meets both classrooms' learning targets.

4. Plan with your partner teacher for how the online video chat will unfold. Who will talk first? What will you do if there is a poor connection? How will you invite students to participate? Consider writing an open-ended script that will guide each class.

5. Prior to connecting through an online video chat, discuss rules and expectations for the chat with students (such as the need to raise their hand, look at the camera and not the display when speaking, and speak loudly and slowly). Remind students they may have technical problems during the

conversation that cause a loss of video signal, garbled audio, and so on.

6. Have students share their learning and collaborate with students in other grade levels, subject areas, or buildings through a simple online, real-time video discussion. When it's over, have a discussion with your class to reflect on what they learned about communicating in this way.

Connections

You can apply this lesson to different content areas in the following ways.

- **English language arts:** With another teacher, connect students in two different classrooms and grade levels that investigate the same genre, such as fairy tales. Connected classrooms could be in the K–2 band or, if you are looking for more of a mentoring role for your students, try to connect with an upper-grade classroom. Students from the higher-grade-level classroom perform a reader's theater activity, reading aloud a story for the lower-grade-level students. The younger students use drawing apps, such as Canva (www.canva.com), to draw pictures of the story they hear the other class perform. This activity enhances the older students' fluency and speaking and listening skills and works on the younger students' visualizing and listening skills.

- **Mathematics:** Connect with a teacher in a different classroom in the same school or in a different school, and plan a lesson on mathematics logic problems. Students in different grade levels or schools join the same sharing platform, such as Seesaw, Kidblog, Edmodo, or Google Classroom. Students or groups of students all post videos or pictures to the sharing platform showing how they solved the same mathematics problem. Teachers and students then use a video chat to discuss the different ways to solve a mathematics problem.

TEACHING TIP

Allow students time to act silly in front of the video-chat camera. Have the camera on for a few minutes before you connect with the other class. It excites elementary students to see themselves on camera just as much as it does to see other students. By letting them act a little goofy beforehand, you will ready them to listen and behave when you connect with the other classroom.

TEACHING TIP

Global Read Aloud (https://theglobalreadaloud.com) gives classrooms a fun way to connect across the globe. This website provides many ways to ensure read-aloud activities connect to your grade-level standards.

TEACHING TIP

Invite students' parents to join online conversations. A classroom could connect with a parent at his or her workplace (especially if it connects with your curriculum), and the parent could virtually join the classroom community through online video conferencing.

Learning goal:
I can use digital tools to communicate and connect with an authentic and live global audience.

Wow: Learning With a Live Global Audience

Connecting with a live, global audience can lead to powerful learning as students absorb diverse perspectives that they may not be accustomed to. This can lead to powerful discussions, and a more complete worldview as students get older. Such a global view may start as a connection to another area in the school district or state and then graduate to a connection across the world. Thematic units, such as holidays around the world, are good opportunities to open K–2 students to worldwide connections. In this lesson, you will make an online connection with another teacher and create collaborative student lessons that correspond to your classroom's learning targets. For this lesson process, we focus on using the free tool Skype in the Classroom (https://education .microsoft.com/skype-in-the-classroom) to make contact with other educators, but if you have a different means to make this connection that you prefer, you can easily adapt this process as you prefer.

Process: Connecting With a Global Classroom

Use the following five steps to establish a global partner classroom.

1. Access the Skype in the Classroom website. Under the Educators tab, select Educator community and then Connect and share with educators. Here you will find teachers that are interested in connecting with other teachers. Some of the teachers are located in the United States, while other teachers are in different parts of the world. Note that the website already calculates time zone differences making it easier for you to assess a teacher partner's availability. Find a partner classroom for your class to connect with based on common learning targets.

2. Work with your partner teacher to find a common theme in the curricula that meets both classrooms' learning targets.

3. Plan with your partner teacher for how the online video chat will unfold. Make sure you address any

potential barriers, such as time differences, language difficulties, and so on.

4. Prior to connecting with the partner classroom online, discuss with students any differences they may notice between the two classrooms. Explain cultural differences, and model showing respect to them. Remind students they may have technical problems during the conversation that cause a loss of video signal, garbled audio, and so on.

5. Have the two classrooms' students share their learning and collaborate with each other while learning about differences between their school cultures. When it's over, have a discussion with your class to reflect on what they learned about communicating in this way.

Connections

You can apply this lesson to different content areas in the following ways.

- **English language arts:** After you find a partner classroom outside your school and decide on a common read-aloud, have each classroom read the story independently from the other. After the classrooms finish reading it, have the classrooms contact each other via video chat using tools like Skype, Google Hangouts, or FaceTime. Facilitate a student discussion about the story components, such as the setting, characters, storyline, and author's purpose. Each classroom can make connections to the story from their lives and the classrooms can compare connections, as they may be different depending on the region in which they live. For example, students in Chicago may have a different version of the Three Little Pigs story than students in Spain do.

- **Mathematics:** After you find a partner classroom to work with, you and your partner teacher communicate to decide on common learning targets. For example, one classroom learns about measurement independently, while the other

TEACHING TIP

Predetermine a time to practice doing this video chat activity with the partner teacher while students are not present. See how well it works and troubleshoot any problems before trying it with the entire class.

DISCUSSION QUESTIONS

Consider the following questions for personal reflection or in collaborative work with colleagues.

▶ What level of understanding did you have of ways for students to share content and collaborate before reading this chapter? What level of understanding do you have now?

▶ How could you use a flipped video lesson to enhance student learning in a lesson you already teach?

▶ How can flipped video lessons help students have strong, independent learning experiences? Would you try using these in independent learning centers in your classroom, and why is this the case?

▶ How does creating a flipped video demonstrate a student's understanding of a concept or skill?

continued ▶

- How does students sharing work using an asynchronous platform, like social media, empower them to learn?

- How can creating a PLN with your teaching peers help you connect with other classrooms locally or globally?

- How does sharing through a blog help students better understand themselves and the world?

- How can a teacher or student creating social media posts have a positive impact on student learning?

- How does establishing a live online connection between classrooms impact student learning? What makes the process and learning different from connecting via a non-live platform like social media?

- How can student feedback provide a learning experience for both the student receiving the feedback and the student giving the feedback?

classroom learns about telling time. Students work collaboratively to decide on teaching points to teach the partner classroom. With guidance, students then contact the partner classroom and teach the topic lesson they have mastered. Students can also give a real-life connection to this mathematics concept based on where they live. For example, if they are in London, they may discuss the historical importance of the iconic Big Ben bell tower. If they are talking about measurement, students may compare the U.S. standard measurement system to the metric system. By connecting students globally, both ends of the connection gain a clearer view of the world and its peoples.

Conclusion

Establishing ways for students to share work and ideas with their peers—not just those in their own classroom or school but others around the world—develops a real sense of digital citizenship and exposes students to new concepts and ideas. In chapter 4, we discuss the importance of teaching K–2 students research skills that will last them a lifetime.

Conducting Research and Curating Information

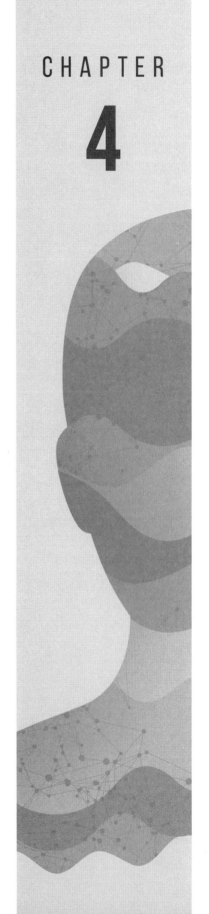

At a young age, students learn that they can find nearly any answer to a question on the Internet. When students ask questions that stump teachers, teachers commonly respond, "I don't know, but let's find out!" With Internet resources available, students and their teachers can research just about any learning inquiry.

As students become confident using devices, they learn how to think critically and gather information through technology. According to noted researcher Chip Donohue (2015), critical thinking is a life skill that drives student inquiry. Teaching our students to research properly gives them an essential digital skill that allows them to become functional digital citizens and leaders (Donohue, 2015).

In this chapter, you will learn how to help students develop into what ISTE refers to as *knowledge constructors*. ISTE (2016) defines knowledge constructors as students who can "critically curate a variety of resources using digital tools to construct knowledge, produce creative artifacts and make meaningful learning experiences for themselves and others." Although this may seem challenging for young students, using technology makes it entirely possible.

Elementary students must learn that finding information online gives them one of the quickest ways to answer a learning inquiry and allows all people to access a wealth of information from a single device. One of the easiest ways for students to start seeing how to gather information is to investigate familiar topics that they already understand. You can then organize students into small groups and use guided practice to bridge them into researching new information. Even the youngest students, including those not able to spell yet, can use the voice search feature most devices include to ask their questions and obtain their answers.

We find it important to help students learn to think critically about the validity of online resources by modeling appropriate website use. We start with a simple lesson to help students decipher between fiction and nonfiction information for research purposes. Before you set students free to work independently or collaboratively with support, students will locate information on sites you provide. Last, students will choose the best resources available to creatively complete a research project. At this chapter's conclusion, you will know how to help students find information in an effective and safe way that helps them become true knowledge constructors.

Gathering and Evaluating Information

Young students have an excitement about learning that is invigorating. Putting the ability to research new topics in their hands allows students to fuel their education and exploration of the world. With some guidance and support from teachers or other adults, students in kindergarten and first and second grade can gather new information on the Internet. As they learn to effectively use search engines, we want to make sure that our students have a safe and structured way to explore new concepts. In the following lessons, we show you how to make digitally gathering and evaluating information come alive.

Novice: Knowing the Difference Between Fiction and Nonfiction When Researching

Students need to understand fiction and nonfiction to properly conduct online research for a project. The ability to organize what content is "real" and what is "not real" helps students construct new understandings. To prepare them, model for students how to compare fiction and nonfiction resources, and discuss the differences between them. For example, if students are researching polar bears and they find a video of a polar bear cartoon, we want those students to be able to understand that polar bears do not talk, even though the polar bear in the video is talking.

Process: Determining a Resource Type

Use the following four steps to help students differentiate between fiction and nonfiction resources.

1. Select a topic that allows students to compare fiction and nonfiction resources.

2. Read and show students examples of both resource types.

3. Complete a graphic organizer with the class comparing the information from the resources (see figure 4.1, page 78).

4. As a class, discuss the graphic organizer in detail, clarifying why a nonfiction resource is more appropriate for a research project. For example, in nonfiction resources, you can find facts, you can answer questions, and you can view real photographs and illustrations on the topic.

Connections

You can apply this lesson to different content areas in the following ways.

-   **English language arts:** Find two videos to compare—one fiction and one nonfiction. For example, when researching penguins, find a fiction video (perhaps a fictional read-aloud with a penguin as a character) and a nonfiction video about penguins (try http://a-z-animals.com/animals). After

Learning goal:
I can understand the difference between fiction and nonfiction information for research purposes.

Name: _____   Did I find true information?

Topic: Penguins

Source: Tacky the Penguin

Source: Real penguins

· Penguins live in Antarctica—"icy land." · Penguins live together. · Penguins march. · Penguins dive. · Penguins swim. · Penguins are birds. · Penguins have feathers and beaks.	· Penguins live in cold and icy Antarctica. · Penguins are birds. · Penguins cannot fly. · Penguins can walk. · Penguins can swim. · Penguins have beaks and feathers and lay eggs. · Penguins communicate with sounds. · Penguins slide on their bellies. · People hunt penguins. · Penguins' animal predators are seals, sea lions, and orcas.	True
· Penguins do not have human names. · Penguins and animals do not talk. · Penguins do not count when they march. · Penguins do not communicate with words. · Penguins' animal predators are not wolves and bears. · Penguins' animal predators do not catch penguins in cages and nets. · Predators do not listen to penguins that don't want to be eaten. · Penguins do not wear clothes. · Penguins do not hit.	· Penguins do not wear sweaters because they have blubber.	Not True

Source: Kirstin McGinnis ©2016

Figure 4.1: Classroom example of students comparing fiction and nonfiction information.

the videos, fill in a comparative chart, like figure 4.1, with students comparing fictional and real penguins.

- **Social studies:** When learning about people within the local or wider community, read related fiction and nonfiction texts. Discuss with students how community helpers in nonfiction texts compare to those in fiction texts.

Operational: Using Online Resources to Gather Information

When students understand the concepts of fiction and non-fiction, you can then model how to research a desired topic using websites or device applications. Some useful sites include PebbleGo (www.pebblego.com), World Book Online (www .worldbookonline.com), Animals A–Z (http://a-z-animals .com), and YouTube Kids (https://kids.youtube.com). (PebbleGo and World Book Online are paid services.) You can also use Symbaloo (www.symbaloo.com) to create and organize a single page students can use to access a variety of safe search tools that you select.

As they become comfortable with these teacher-provided tools or search engines, students can use them to conduct their research, record their research findings, and begin a research-based writing piece. Younger students can conduct research online and then use drawing and labels in paper journals to describe their findings. Note that a lack of literacy skills should not deter you or your students in finding out new information. To aid your students, you might consider writing searchable words on chart paper and helping students type those words, such as we wrote about in chapter 1. Or, try having students use a voice-search option, which is available in the YouTube Kids app. As your classroom practices these research skills, they will become more and more fluent with the skill!

Our youngest students will need quite a bit of support to access online material that aligns with the learning target, which is why we suggest using safe search engines and QR codes that link to appropriate sites. However, despite your best efforts, students may access links with content that is not age-appropriate or is otherwise unhelpful for the task at

Learning goal:
I can locate information using a website or app the teacher provides.

hand. When this happens, review appropriate use and use those moments to teach the importance of filtering out negative and off-topic information.

Process: Gathering Information

Use the following five steps to have students pick a topic and gather information on it.

1. Have students select a desired learning topic related to your curriculum.

2. Tell students to choose a search engine or app from a list of options that you provide and then choose search terms related to the topic.

3. Have students use their search results to research information on their topic for about ten minutes. During this time, assist students in navigating toward the right content. If you have classroom tech-sperts for conducting Internet searches, have them work with their peers as well.

4. Using chart paper, model for the full class how to organize what students learn. We suggest using a KWL (what I know, what I wonder, what I learned) chart to start with.

5. Model how to take organized information and write a grade-level-appropriate informational paragraph as a class. Students who would like to expand could do so individually in their journal at another time.

Connections

You can apply this lesson to different content areas in the following ways.

- **English language arts:** Ask students to work collaboratively with a partner and choose a topic to research. Use YouTube Kids or set up a custom Symbaloo page with selected search engines to have students locate information on an assigned topic. Once students master locating appropriate information with the resources you provide, they can move on to locating information on their own.

- **Science:** Have students work with partners or individually to research plant life cycles. Students

---

TECH TIP

Show students two search options: voice search and text search. If you choose to use voice search with students, make sure students know how to enable voice search on their devices.

TECH TIP

You can read a NOW Classrooms blog entry with pictures and more lesson ideas for using YouTube Kids and Symbaloo (http://nowclassrooms.com/symbaloo-for-organization-and-safe-searching).

may either type in or use voice search to research terms such as *plant life cycle, how plants grow*, or *what plants need to live*. After they find videos or read digital books on the topic, students should use scratch paper or a journal to jot down notes or draw illustrations that reflect what they learned.

Wow: Choosing Resources Independently

Even student-focused search engines generate nearly infinite results for students to select from. When students have learned to use basic search engine features, they should then develop their understanding of how to choose among the resources in their search results. For students ready to take the next step in their online research, you can model for them and support them in learning how to choose the resources that best meet their needs. Learning to filter out extraneous and unreliable information is an important 21st century skill that lays the groundwork for students' future abilities to distinguish between rich and poor content.

For this lesson, you will create a Symbaloo (www.symbaloo.com) page of resources or assemble a collection of QR codes that students can use to independently research and write about a topic. You will find Symbaloo particularly handy for this purpose because it allows you to restrict the research tools students access to only those you consider appropriate.

Process: Gathering Research Sources

Use the following five steps to curate a list of sources students can use for research.

1. As a class, develop a list of websites appropriate for a research topic you have selected.

2. Use Symbaloo or QR codes to create a collection of links to those websites.

3. Tell students to choose the websites they want to use for their research by clicking on the Symbaloo tiles or scanning the QR codes.

4. Ask students to use their research abilities to write on the research topic. Their research process may

Learning goal:
I can choose from a variety of apps and websites to find what resources best meet my needs to independently, or with support, complete a research project.

DISCUSSION QUESTIONS

Consider the following questions for personal reflection or in collaborative work with colleagues.

▸ What level of understanding of student-friendly research sources did you have before reading this chapter? What level of understanding do you have after reading it?

▸ Why do K–2 students need to understand the differences between fiction and nonfiction before you have them research a topic?

▸ How does receiving teacher guidance on locating research information help teach students about the validity of online resources?

▸ How would you redirect a student who finds an inappropriate website or a website that does not provide desired information?

▸ In what ways is using technology similar to using books when it comes to finding research information? How does technology make research information more accessible to all students?

▸ Why is having the ability to independently choose their research sources an important skill to teach students?

continued ▸

look similar to figure 4.2, but use a process that best fits your class's needs.

5. Have students post their research project to your LMS or social media site.

Figure 4.2: Students demonstrating the research process from beginning to end.

Connections

You can apply this lesson to different content areas in the following ways.

- **English language arts:** Have students open the Symbaloo page at www.symbaloo.com /mix/kidsresearchtools, where they will find numerous search engines and websites they can use to safely research topics. (Some of these are paid sites.) Prompt students to use tiles on the Symbaloo page to explore a literacy topic that your class investigates. After a couple of minutes of exploration time, pull the students together as a whole group to discuss what type of information each website provides (fiction or nonfiction) and record these results on chart paper. Discuss what website they could best use as a source of research on the topic.

- **Mathematics:** Use a set of approximately ten QR codes that link to flipped videos students have made in the past, or that other classes have made, that explain how to measure with different objects. Or, provide students with QR codes that link to digitally published videos about measurement. Have them use these QR code videos to research how to measure. Students should decide which videos are most helpful to them in building an understanding of measurement.

Conclusion

In this chapter, you learned some practical methods for exposing students to age-appropriate search engines they can use as they learn how to research topics you assign or topics that they self-generate. The lessons in chapter 5 build on this knowledge by offering lessons you can use to develop students' critical-thinking, problem-solving, and project-management abilities.

▸ How do students' website-research choices help a teacher assess their ability to appropriately use technology?

▸ What additional safety measures can you take to ensure that students stay safe on the Internet when doing research?

▸ What units that you teach would benefit from technology-backed research? Share them on social media with the hashtag #NOWClassrooms.

Thinking Critically to Solve Problems

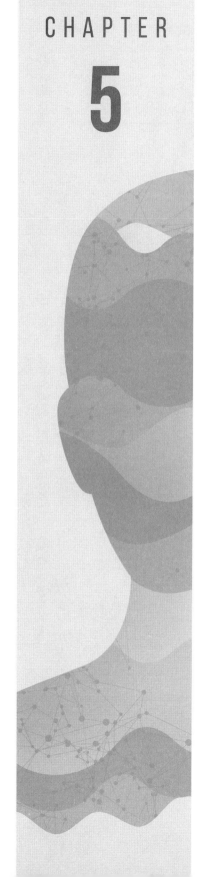

The 2016 ISTE Standards for Students state that each student has the power to become an *innovative designer* and a *computational thinker*. Computational thinkers can find and recognize problems and then develop and carry out solutions. As innovative designers, we hope to develop our students not to just carry out actions, but to innovate while doing so. To that end, this chapter focuses on helping you create lessons that promote critical-thinking, problem-solving, and decision-making skills using technology that allows students to exponentially grow these essential skills both in and out of the classroom. Developing these skills early on in students' academic careers allows them to continuously challenge themselves and innovate at all grade levels.

All students can achieve in these areas. In an article published in the *Association for the Advancement of Computing in Education Journal*, researchers Jared Keengwe, Grace Onchwari, and Jacqueline Onchwari (2009) state they believe teachers must "Develop learning tasks that actively engage [students] and help them to develop higher-order skills such as problem-solving and critical-thinking skills" (p. 12). Students who explore and play with various technology tools early on in their education learn how to choose appropriate digital tools to reach their learning goals as they grow up. When students can demonstrate their learning in a meaningful way, learning becomes more personalized and much deeper.

In this chapter, we offer lessons to help you improve students' abilities to think critically, problem solve, and make decisions while using technology in a meaningful way. By choosing appropriate tools and learning how to plan and manage a project, students will begin to fully understand how to develop computational-thinking skills.

Planning and Producing Using Digital Tools

For a long time, teachers could only use tests to assess what students learned in the classroom, but in the 21st century, teachers have many more ways to gauge students' knowledge acquisition. What would happen if you asked your students to show what they know instead of having them take a pencil-and-paper test? Would they know how to demonstrate their understanding in a more personalized way? Could your students teach others?

When we give students a problem that they have not seen before, we want to know that they can work out a solution because the world expects 21st century learners to demonstrate their ability through action, not filling in bubbles on a standardized test. According to the Pew Research Center, as algorithms and artificial intelligence are increasingly involved in almost every field, the jobs of the future need workers with critical-thinking and problem-solving skills like never before (Rainie & Anderson, 2017).

Throughout the *NOW Classrooms* series, we emphasize the importance of student voice and choice, meaning that students select the digital tools and the process to demonstrate what they learn. Young students especially need to start building experience with different digital tools, so they can make better-informed choices about what will best help them accomplish a learning target. So, the goal of this NOW lesson set is to give students opportunities to explore and play with different digital tools so they can begin building these kinds of skills. Once they have a chance to do this, you can begin to teach students how different digital tools can provide choice in how they creatively demonstrate their learning.

Because these lessons introduce topics that require technology proficiency to achieve the desired outcomes, we recommend that you do not introduce students to these lessons until they have at least operational abilities with most of the previous lessons in this book. As students become more proficient at this chapter's lessons, they will have the ability to identify and choose a digital tool to complete a task or project on their own.

Novice: Learning About Digital Tools

Apps have, in many ways, taken over the digital world because they represent a simple, effective means for accomplishing a specific task. One-size-fits-all applications may let you do a lot, but they typically don't do any one thing very effectively. Apps, more often than not, are also incredibly inexpensive, even free. In an app-driven world, students need to learn that for any given assignment or task, they have different specialized tools available to help them complete it. Likewise, allowing students to choose the tool they want to use to solve problems individualizes student learning and gives them agency in their own learning. Teachers can easily make this accommodation.

This lesson provides you with a framework for introducing students to a variety of apps. This exposure will help them understand how digital tools differ from each other. Note that we don't recommend specific tools for this lesson as you will need to choose the tools that fit your class needs the best. If you want to look for ideas, we suggest using this book's appendix or conducting your own Internet search for tools related to the types of projects you want to conduct in your classroom.

Process: Using a New Digital Tool

Use the following four steps to introduce students to a new digital tool, either one from a previous lesson, or one from the appendix that you would like to try out.

1. Select an app or website that allows students to complete a task related to a learning target.

Learning goal:
I can use a digital tool my teacher provides to complete a task with purpose.

2. Model for the class how to use the app or website. Go over any glitches you may have discovered, any meaningful icons, and the app's purpose and how it relates to classroom learning.

3. Give students ten to fifteen minutes to explore the app or website. During this time, have them sit as a whole group so that you can monitor what is going on as well as address any questions as they arise.

4. Repeat this process for each app or website you introduce, as needed.

Connections

You can apply this lesson to different content areas in the following ways.

- **English language arts:** After practicing written opinion writing as a class, introduce students to digital tools they can choose from to create a final opinion-writing piece. You may provide students with a point to argue or let them self-direct. For example, introduce students to the storybook *Don't Let the Pigeon Drive the Bus!* (Willems, 2003) and then ask them if they believe Pigeon should be able to drive the bus. Have students sit with partners and converse on this question, then call them back together and model using My Storybook (www.mystorybook.com), Book Creator (https://bookcreator.com), and Scholastic Story Starters (www.scholastic.com/teachers/story-starters) to start a digital opinion writing piece on the same topic. Allow students to choose the tool they want to use to write their piece. Upon completion, have them upload their digital-writing piece to the classroom LMS and then share it with parents or peers as you see fit. As a great school-home connection, invite parents into your classroom for an authors' evening so your students can share their digital work.

- **Mathematics:** Allow students to choose an app or website such as Schoolkit Math (www.schoolkitapps.com), 10 Frame Fill (http://bit.ly/2ukimz2), or Explain Everything (https://explaineverything.com) to explain their thinking and processes when solving mathematics problems. For example, you might give students a word problem as part of their morning work or the morning message. Have students use their device to document how they figured out the problem and then share it on the classroom LMS, or have them bring the device and solution to the morning meeting to share with peers.

Operational: Selecting Appropriate Digital Tools From a Menu

As you introduce multiple digital tools to your class, you must teach students what tasks each tool will help them complete. To grow students' ability to make informed selections, practice giving students a menu of app options, like figure 5.1 (page 90), to accomplish a specific task. Then allow students to work in pairs to determine what tool would best help them complete the given task. At higher grade levels, particularly grades 9–12, most students will receive assignments from teachers in which the final product matters more than the process used to achieve it, and students will have to figure out the best way to create it on their own. In conjunction with the research lessons in chapter 4, having students learn these selection skills early better prepares them to do that.

Process: Choosing a Tool From a Menu

Use the following five steps to introduce multiple learning tools to students and allow them to select which one they want to use to accomplish a task.

1. Decide on a learning objective for students to accomplish, and then assemble a menu of digital tools students can use to accomplish it. Students should be able to use any of the tools you provide to accomplish their objective, but do include tools on the menu that are more suitable than others. In this way, you can gauge students' abilities to choose the best tool from the range of options you provided.

2. Introduce the menu of digital tools to the students, going over each one.

3. Allow students time to explore these apps on their own. Students can work in pairs to explore and discuss the tools.

Learning goal:
I can choose the digital tool, from a menu of digital tools my teacher provides, that will help me complete a task.

1:1 Menu / Week 1

Word Work	1. Rover: ABCya. 2. Make a screenshot. 3. Import Educreations. 4. Write sentences.	Educreations Continue working in Educreations.	Make-a-Word Explain Everything 1. Open Dropbox. 2. Click on Make-a-Word. 3. Make five words, and type them out. 4. Read them and record them.
Listening	Raz-Kids	Keynote 1. Open National Geographic Kids. 2. Listen to a nonfiction story. 3. Use Keynote to show what you learned.	Finish up Keynote. Keynote
Reading to Someone	QuickVoice 1. Choose a story from a reading book. 2. Take turns reading. 3. Record it.	Keynote iMovie How will you and your partner retell a story? Choose your app! ArtStudio Book Creator	Stickies 1. Choose a story from a reading book. 2. Open Sticky Notes. 3. Retell the story. 4. Make a screenshot when you're done.
Writing	Kidblog Log in, and respond to my post!	ArtStudio 1. Create a picture. 2. Use a text box: 3. Beginning, middle, and end!	Kidblog 1. Read the responses. 2. Reply to five friends' comments.
Reading to Yourself	QuickVoice 1. Choose a story from a reading book. 2. Record it. 3. Listen to it. 4. Fill out the fluency checklist.	QuickVoice 1. Reread the same story. 2. Record it. 3. Listen to it. 4. Fill out the fluency checklist. 5. Reflect on what you did better, and record.	Keynote iMovie How will you retell the story? Choose your app! ArtStudio Book Creator

Figure 5.1: Sample digital tools menu.

4. Have students individually choose a digital tool from the menu to complete the task.

5. Once students finish their product and either upload it to the classroom LMS or receive your approval, conference with them about their choice and the process that they took. Some students may be ready to choose tools that have many more advanced steps, while others are just trying to finish the task. Ask students, "Did you like working on this project?" "Was it difficult, and why?" "What can you do better next time?"

Connections

You can apply this lesson to different content areas in the following ways.

- **English language arts:** Create a match-the-task lesson, like figure 5.2 (page 92), to model for students how to match tasks with apps and websites you select. Note that this differs from using a menu with multiple apps all suited to the same task in that not all the apps listed will suit all the listed tasks. This creates room for error that will help you gauge students' progress. Have students complete the lesson independently or in pairs.

- **Mathematics:** Create a match-the-task lesson similar to the English language arts connections, but instead use mathematics prompts and connected applications.

Wow: Independently Selecting a Digital Tool to Complete a Task

As students become experts at choosing among multiple digital tools, you can begin to have them work more independently. Give wow-level students a task that allows them to discover for themselves the appropriate digital tool to use to complete it.

Process: Completing a Task Independently With an App

Use the following four steps to assign students a task that they independently complete using an app.

Learning goal:
I can independently identify and choose the best digital tool to use to complete a task.

Match the Task With a Digital Tool	
Match each of the following technology tasks to the app that you find most appropriate to use for that task by drawing a line between them.	
Type three sentences about your favorite food.	Explain Everything
Take a picture of five different shapes in the classroom.	QuickVoice
Record yourself reading your favorite picture book.	Google Docs
Take a picture of five different shapes, and record the name of each shape.	Camera
Take a picture of your favorite shape. Give your shape a voice, and have it talk about what kind of shape it is.	ChatterPix Kids

Figure 5.2: Sample match-the-task activity.

1. Give students a task that they must complete with an app. Although students should have prior exposure to multiple apps that are suited to completing the task, do not recommend specific apps to them for this process.

2. Tell students to choose an appropriate app for completing the task.

3. Ask students to independently complete the task using the app.

4. Have students share their completed work with you via the classroom LMS. You should evaluate the completed assignment using your preferred rubric for the learning target.

Connections

You can apply this lesson to different content areas in the following ways.

- **English language arts:** After learning about sequencing, have students choose an app to use to show the sequence of a story they read, such as Flipagram (https://flipagram.com) or Shadow Puppet Edu (http://get-puppet.co). Students can draw pictures or take pictures of the story and then use their app of choice to put the pictures in the correct order—beginning, middle, and end.

- **Mathematics:** Have students find five different shapes throughout the classroom and then identify the attributes that make each shape the shape it is. Students can use an app of their choice to show what they know about the shapes. They can share their final products on a classroom community wall so all students can see which apps are appropriate for this project.

Managing Projects Independently

A student's ability to plan, manage, and share his or her products makes up an integral part of successful technology integration. This involves broader learning than the relatively simple act of matching a tool to a task. For these lessons, students must know how to determine and sequence the steps necessary to complete a complex multistep task or project. After a teacher models these steps first, students should work in small groups before moving forward to independently plan, manage, and complete tasks on their own. Students will learn to properly manage projects by creating checklists for monitoring their progress. You will scaffold these lessons for students by engaging them in large-group, small-group, and independent work. By creating a stepped sequence to complete the project, and gaining peer and teacher feedback, students will gain ownership and knowledge on how to successfully manage multistep projects.

For these lessons, you can introduce some fantastic resources to students that will help them become familiar with this sort of project management, including Trello (https://trello .com), Notes (www.get-notes.com), Reminders (a default iOS app), Google Docs (https://docs.google.com), and Google Classroom (https://classroom.google.com). For schools subscribed to G Suite for Education, we particularly recommend the web or app version of Google Keep (www.google.com /keep), a great resource for helping students manage due dates and projects.

Regardless of the project-management app or tool you choose, once students reach wow-level proficiency in these lessons, they should know how to complete some of the following multistep tasks.

- Create and share projects, assignments, and work.
- Manage folders in programs such as Google Docs or Google Classroom or similar apps.
- Research, create, and share findings.
- Upload project materials to an LMS platform, such as Seesaw, Showbie, or Google Classroom.

In the past, when working on traditional projects, a teacher might have posted precise, step-by-step directions for students to follow. Through these lessons, you can develop students' digital independence by allowing them more voice and choice in how they complete their work. Successful digital project management takes time and practice, and students will be at different readiness points for these management tools, but with practice even our youngest learners can keep their work organized, building a foundation for future success.

Novice: Following Directions for a Multistep Digital Task

Completing a multistep digital task is vital to success in the classroom. When K–2 students understand and follow multistep directions, they can truly begin to become strong independent learners and creators. Although working independently requires students to understand the steps in a multistep task, at this stage it is beneficial to provide students with a visual direction sheet that you explain and they can reference to complete the task. Figure 5.3 provides an example of a step-by-step visual direction sheet students can use to independently guide themselves, but you could adapt this

Learning goal:

I can follow the directions provided to complete a multistep digital task.

idea to your classroom in plenty of ways. To encourage independence, make yourself available for support, but as much as possible refer students back to the direction sheet.

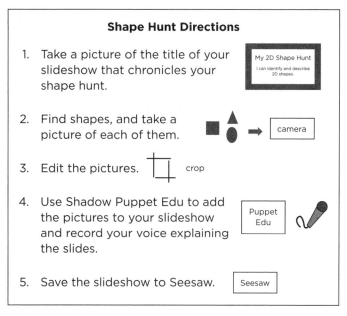

Figure 5.3: Sample classroom step-by-step direction sheet.

Process: Using a Visual Direction Sheet

Use the following four steps to create a visual direction sheet students can use to complete a multistep digital task.

1. Create a visual direction sheet (a paper printout or an anchor chart) with steps students must follow to complete a digital task.

2. When you ask students to use or open a specific app, provide them with a picture of the app in your directions.

3. Display the visual direction sheet in the classroom or in an independent learning center for students to use.

4. Have students complete the desired task by following the visual directions. Students should upload their finished product to the classroom LMS for you to evaluate using your preferred rubric.

Connections

You can apply this lesson to different content areas in the following ways.

- **English language arts:** Create a sample visual direction sheet to guide students in explaining the sequence of a story. Read the story to students and review with them its beginning, middle, and end. Have students draw a picture in their writing journal with pencil and paper retelling the three main parts of the story. They should then use their devices to take pictures of their drawings and create a slideshow that includes a title, as well as their pictures retelling the beginning, middle, and end of the story. For added sophistication, have students record audio discussing or narrating their pictures. They should upload their completed products to the classroom LMS for you to review and evaluate.

- **Mathematics:** Have students follow a visual direction sheet that you created to find shapes around the classroom. Students should use digital tools to add the shapes they found to a slideshow application and then record their voice talking about how and where they found the shapes. Students should upload their completed products to the classroom LMS for you to review and evaluate.

Operational: Completing a Multistep Task in a Small Group

Learning goal:
I can determine and sequence the steps needed to complete a multistep task with a small group.

When students can follow visual directions that you provide, the next step is to have them develop their own steps for completing a task. This benefits students by requiring them to use their own critical-thinking skills to plan and execute a given task in a small group setting. As part of this process, it is important to review with students your expectations for how they will collaborate. This may be something as simple as ensuring students understand the importance of listening to all voices in the group, making eye contact when speaking, and taking turns. Reviewing these expectations with students helps ensure a collaborative product that models true student achievement and understanding of a subject. During small group work, teachers should be monitoring and helping facilitate problem-solving skills among the groups.

Process: Creating a Checklist

Use the following four steps to have students create a checklist for completing a multistep task.

1. Give students a multistep task to complete.

2. In small groups, instruct students to plan for what they need to accomplish in the task by brainstorming a checklist.

3. Have students use a word-processing or record-keeping program like Google Docs or Google Keep to create a checklist for what they need to accomplish.

4. Once students complete their checklist of necessary tasks, have them share their final checklist with you via the classroom LMS. Once you review and approve their checklists, have them proceed with their project.

Connections

You can apply this lesson to different content areas in the following ways.

- **Social studies:** Assign student groups to work on a nonfiction research project related to a geography-themed topic, such as identifying different topographical land formations. Review with students group expectations and have them work together to create a list of important tasks they need to complete to successfully accomplish their research goals.

- **Mathematics:** Have student groups practice reading and interpreting a graph or other data source. Select topics for students to collect data on, such as favorite colors, favorite foods, number of family members, and so on. Student groups should determine the steps required to gather the data they need and then create a graph. Each group will build a checklist to demonstrate how they can work collaboratively to accomplish the task and then upload it to the classroom LMS for your review and approval prior to starting their project.

Wow: Independently Sequencing a Multistep Task

Students who master determining and sequencing steps to complete a multistep task can expand their skill set to include independently planning their own task, recording their ideas, and then sharing their steps with other students and you. This process helps students determine the appropriateness of their independently created plan of action to complete a task and builds a foundation for students to better process, plan, and think through a multistep task.

Process: Recording a Multistep Plan

Use the following five steps to have students record and present their sequence of steps for a multistep task.

1. Assign students a multistep task related to a classroom learning target.

2. Have students independently create a plan for the learning target and create a list of sequential steps they will use to complete the project.

3. To gain valuable feedback, ask students to share their multistep task list with a partner and consider feedback for editing as necessary.

4. After revising their checklists to ensure they convey their understanding of the learning target, have students share their checklists with you via the classroom LMS.

5. Have students use their multistep task lists to complete their projects.

Connections

You can apply this lesson to different content areas in the following ways.

- **English language arts:** After reading a nonfiction story, have students individually create a multistep plan to retell the story using a digital tool of their choice. Each student should brainstorm his or her plan and get approval for it from you before he or

Learning goal:

I can independently determine and sequence the steps needed to complete a multistep task.

DISCUSSION QUESTIONS

Consider the following questions for personal reflection or in collaborative work with colleagues.

▸ What understanding of the importance of teaching students to make independent choices did you have before reading this chapter? What is your biggest takeaway from this chapter?

▸ Why do you need to model for K–2 students how to properly use a website or use a learning game or app?

▸ Why do you need to guide students to use the proper application or website to complete a task or activity? Why is it important to practice this technology skill in isolation?

continued ▸

she proceeds. After creating his or her final project, share it with another class to receive feedback. Have students write a reflective summary on their feedback noting how they could improve their multistep plans to form a better final product.

- **Mathematics:** Have students brainstorm a plan to break down a complex word problem into multiple steps and then record their plan in a digital document. Have students share their plan with a partner to see if it helps their partner to solve the problem. After receiving feedback from their partner, students should reflect on how they could improve their multistep plan.

Conclusion

In this chapter, you learned important classroom lessons that will engage students in their learning by giving them choices and ownership over the means and steps they use to complete projects. The project-management lessons in this chapter will form solid foundational knowledge your students can take with them throughout their scholastic and professional careers. In chapter 6, we begin the important process of helping students understand what it means to be a good digital citizen.

▶ In what ways could an activity like *match the task* have value in your classroom? Please provide some examples.

▶ Why is student-led digital creation highly valuable?

▶ What similarities does managing projects with technology have with managing projects without technology? How does technology make project management easier?

▶ Why are classroom management, social skills, and collaboration important for a multistep technology planning process?

▶ How can students use technology to help them manage their time as they plan a project?

▶ How does allowing students to manage a project on their own empower their learning?

▶ Do you have a project or activity you use that you can manage in a more meaningful way after reading this chapter? Share it with your PLN on Twitter using the #NOWClassrooms hashtag.

Being Responsible Digital Citizens

Multiple times during a school year, students and teachers practice fire, tornado, and intruder drills. Many teachers invite local police and fire departments to their schools to teach students about personal and community safety. As our society evolves into an increasingly digital world, Mike Ribble (2011) says in his book *Digital Citizenship in Schools*:

> It is our responsibility to provide all users the opportunity to work, interact, and use technology without interference, destruction, or obstruction by the actions of inappropriate users. Good digital citizens work to help create a society of users who help others learn how to use technology appropriately. (p. 12)

As teachers, we have the responsibility to teach students how to stay safe as well as become good citizens in online communities. We recommend familiarizing yourself with the Children's Online Privacy Protection Act of 1998 and any digital protection documents that your district may have.

All stakeholders, including parents, students, and teachers, should make creating responsible digital citizens a priority (Crockett & Churches, 2018). ISTE (2016) states that good digital citizens "recognize the rights, responsibilities and opportunities of living, learning and working in an interconnected digital world, and they act and model in ways that are safe, legal, and ethical." Teaching Internet responsibility, or *digital citizenship*, plays a crucial part in online learning, especially for K–2 students who are learning social norms both in the physical and digital worlds.

Even though K–2 students do not know a world without the Internet, that does not mean they are good digital citizens. These are concepts we need to help them with every time they use a digital device regardless of the academic content we are focusing on. Teachers must explicitly teach and model expectations to help students understand the importance of behaving legally and ethically while online. As students become more detailed in their research and references, they must also understand how to properly acknowledge the work they use, as well as their own work.

In this chapter, we offer lessons about creating digital citizens, specifically, personal safety, online stranger danger, and cyberbullying. We also provide lessons that help students understand the importance of creating original work and including an age-appropriate list of the sources they use for projects. For a student generation that spends as much time online as offline, we must make sure students become good digital citizens that know how to properly respect and protect data.

Creating Digital Citizens

The broad topic of digital citizenship varies, depending on the content that students have access to and students' ages. You have many resources online for teaching and learning about digital citizenship. The following resources have age-appropriate ways of learning about digital citizenship, and a few of them have their own curricula: Kahoot! Online Safety (http://bit.ly/2nVKwgC), BrainPOP Jr.'s Internet Safety course (http://bit.ly/1J9CHaI), ABCya's Cyber-Five (http://bit.ly/18XpaXW), and Common Sense Education (www.commonsense.org/education).

Teaching K–2 students digital citizenship begins with teaching them how to conduct themselves responsibly and safely in the physical world and then while online. Teachers must explicitly teach social norms and model positive behavior in class and then connect that to positive online behavior. This includes teaching students about how to respond to stranger danger and bullying, how to deal with strangers they might encounter online, and how to report behavior that troubles them or makes them feel unsafe. It is imperative to start teaching these lessons as soon as students start using digital tools so that they can protect themselves and develop into confident and appropriate digital citizens.

Novice: Staying Safe Online

In this lesson, you will help students begin to understand the importance of staying safe online by creating a social story about stranger danger and bullying. Most students in this age group have some understanding that they should beware of strangers and bullying in the physical world. Use that knowledge to facilitate a discussion about the online equivalent of strangers and bullying to address how they also threaten students' safety in the digital world.

Process: Introducing Stranger Danger and Cyberbullying

Use the following five steps to educate students on how to stay safe online.

1. In a whole-group discussion, use an anchor chart or social story to identify and describe a bully or stranger to your students.

2. Discuss how bullies act in real life and ways that students can keep themselves and others safe from harm in the physical world. What do bullies say? How do bullies make you feel? How should you report bullying? What are some ways we can help others who are being bullied?

3. Have a class discussion on how bullies act online and ways that students can keep themselves and others safe from harm online. What might bullies say online? How would they make you feel? How should you report online bullying? Why is it important to report online bullying?

TEACHING TIP

In your newsletters home, let parents know you discuss digital citizenship at school, what it is, and how they can become digital role models for their students.

Learning goal:
I can understand personal online safety.

4. Create an anchor chart comparing bullies online and in real life and post it in the classroom.

5. Continue to revisit and discuss the anchor chart over several weeks before going online to help create safe habits. If bullying issues arise online or in the classroom, review the chart with your students as needed.

Connections

You can apply this lesson to different content areas in the following ways.

- **English language arts:** With your students, read a social story on bullying prevention, such as *One* by Kathryn Otoshi (2008). After reading it, divide a piece of chart paper in half using a marker. Label one side of this anchor chart *Online* and the other side *Real Life*, as shown in figure 6.1. Identify and describe how the bully in the story acts and if people act like that in real life. Discuss what a bully looks like and sounds like and how he or she makes you feel. Write down students' comments on the Real Life side. On a separate piece of chart paper, do the same thing to describe what a stranger looks and sounds like and makes students feel like. Then connect bullying to the virtual world by talking about how people can do and say mean things through their device as well. Fill in the Online side of each piece of chart paper with your students, discussing what a bully and a stranger look like online. Discuss with students that when they feel unsafe or hurt at home or at school, they should tell an adult, and they can do the same thing when they feel unsafe or hurt when using their device.

- **Social science:** Lead a class discussion about a current event where bullying is involved. A good source for searching for age-appropriate news is on the website Newsela (https://newsela.com).

Figure 6.1: Sample anchor chart describing real-life and online bullies.

Operational: Protecting Personal Data From Strangers

The next step in the development of digital citizenship has students go from having awareness of others' behavior online to having awareness of their own. This lesson is designed to help students understand what information they should and should not put on the Internet and how to deal with strangers who ask for that information. For this lesson, create an anchor chart, like figure 6.2 (page 106), and facilitate a discussion about what personal information to protect and why students need to keep it private.

Learning goal:
I can keep my personal data safe from strangers online.

Figure 6.2: Sample anchor chart on keeping personal information safe.

Process: Protecting Your Information

Use the following three steps to teach students how to protect their information.

1. Review the anchor chart with students. Discuss what strangers may look or sound like in an online community. Do they say mean things? Do they ask for personal information? Do they make others sad or mad?

2. Discuss what personal information students should keep safe from strangers online, such as their name, phone number, birthday, address, school, family members, and age. Solicit ideas for this list from your students, and list them on the anchor chart.

3. Discuss and make a plan for what students should immediately do if a stranger or bully makes them or a friend feel threatened, scared, or uncomfortable online because of the information he or she asks for.

Connections

You can apply this lesson to different content areas in the following ways.

- **Social science:** Use Google Maps (https://maps
.google.com) and street names (without address
numbers) to map out where students live in relation
to school. Discuss that this is an appropriate activity
to do in class. For example, you could say, "We
can share this information here because we are all
friends, but we would never share this information
online because only your friends and family should
know where you live." Strangers should not know
where you live unless an adult has given them
permission.

- **Mathematics:** Use the website Internet Live Stats
(www.internetlivestats.com/watch/internet-users) to
lead a discussion about how many people are on the
Internet all over the globe and what that means for
student safety.

Wow: Putting a Stop to Cyberbullying

At this point, your students have awareness of stranger danger, cyberbullying behavior, and the importance of protecting
their personal information. Students at this level should also
have some knowledge of how to report behavior that makes
them feel threatened or uncomfortable. The novice and
operational lessons for this topic help make students aware
of toxic online behavior; however, understanding these dangers isn't the same as having these dangers confront them.
As a teacher, you must help students understand these issues
using concrete examples. You may want to draft an example of a toxic online conversation and ask students how they
would converse differently. Discuss appropriate commenting
on uploaded work (as we cover in chapter 3), how to respond
to negative comments, and what to do if a stranger comments. Further, talk about how to safely report to a respected
adult incidences of cyberbullying or encounters with strangers. Checking in with an adult about the appropriateness of
digital content is always OK, and the sooner students come
to adults, the better. You can illustrate these responses using
an anchor chart, like figure 6.3 (page 108).

Learning goal:
I can identify
cyberbullying
and report it.

Figure 6.3: Sample anchor chart for putting a stop to bullying.

Process: Stopping a Cyberbully

Use the following five steps to help students identify and put a stop to a cyberbully.

1. Discuss specific ways that a cyberbully might behave or sound when bullying a student in an online community. What things do cyberbullies say? How do cyberbullies make you feel? What words might they use?

2. Discuss what students should do immediately if they feel threatened, scared, or uncomfortable based on online information. Whom can they talk to about cyberbullying?

3. Provide students with a safe space to anonymously report bullying. You may want to consider having a notepad, pen, and jar somewhere in your classroom for students to leave you anonymous notes. You could also provide means for students to privately report bullying via your classroom LMS.

4. Commend any recognition of cyberbullying as it appears. "I am so proud of Stella for letting me know that someone was being unkind with his or

her words on her Seesaw project. I have removed the unkind comments, and I think we should talk more about how to leave positive feedback." Sharing examples like this with students are powerful teachable moments within the classroom.

5. Continue to review cyberbullying issues and respond to cyberbullying in the same manner as the year progresses.

Connections

You can apply this lesson to different content areas in the following ways.

*   **English language arts:** Use the music video "Pause and Think Online" from the Common Sense Media website (www.commonsensemedia.org /pause) to spark a conversation about cyberbullying. You can also create and hand out small versions or bookmarks of an online safety anchor chart you make as a class for students to reference when they encounter cyberbullying (see figure 6.4, page 110).

*   **Mathematics:** As a whole class, lead a discussion about the infographic *What happens online in 60 seconds?* (http://bit.ly/2v0Z5Xx; Allen, 2017). Talk with students about the volume of data the infographic represents, how many people it represents, and why this makes demonstrating good digital citizenship and being aware of how to deal with online bullying so important.

Understanding Creative Work and Intellectual Property

As students collaborate and learn how to safely find information online, they must learn how to properly share their own original work and respect others' original work as well. Because K–2 students naturally emulate others, it is vital that they learn and understand how to be independent with regard to their writing and artwork. Creating their own work that they are proud of, while respecting and recognizing the work that others have created, is a good social norm to be

> **TEACHING TIP**
>
> Set up a safe classroom process for reporting cyberbullying. This could involve something as easy as having an empty tissue box in which students can leave their concerns written on slips of paper for you to review. Or, tell your students that they can message you through your classroom LMS to report anything that makes them uncomfortable.

Source: Adapted from Common Sense Media, 2014.

Figure 6.4: Sample teacher-created student bookmark on online safety.

aware of both in life and in the digital community. As students complete projects of increasing difficulty, help them learn the importance of clearly and concisely citing information sources that they use.

Novice: Labeling Work Online

Students at this age think of ownership as an abstract concept, but you have practical ways to help them begin to understand ownership and respect the ownership of others in your classroom. This process begins with establishing for them the value of work. This lesson has students create a product for you to pass to one of their peers. Through role playing and teacher-led discussion, students will learn how it feels for someone else to get credit for their work. Use this

Learning goal:

I can understand that putting my name on my projects labels them as mine.

lesson to help students understand ownership in a meaningful way.

Process: Learning the Value of Ownership

Use the following eight steps to have students create work and learn the value of ownership.

1. Have students each draw a picture on a piece of paper. Instruct the students not to put their name on their drawing.

2. Collect the papers, and mix them up.

3. Pass back a drawing to each student, trying to make sure each student does not get his or her own artwork.

4. Once all students have a drawing, give positive feedback on the artwork that each student has, as if it is the work of the student now holding it. Expect to hear complaints such as, "Hey, that is mine!"

5. Ask students how it makes them feel to hear others get credit for their work. For example, ask, "Kaliyah, how did it make you feel that I told Devon I loved the picture that you drew?"

6. Foster a conversation with your students on how getting and taking credit for someone else's work hurts that person's feelings and why it is not right.

7. Give students back their original artwork, and instruct them to put their name on it.

8. Discuss the importance of not only putting your name on your own work but also giving credit to the person who made a different piece of work.

Connections

You can apply this lesson to different content areas in the following ways.

- **English language arts:** When reading a storybook to students, discuss the author and illustrator of the book. Ask them, "Why do you think they put their names on the cover?" and "Do you think that they feel proud of their work?" Focus on teaching students why they should give themselves credit for the work they do. Use the "My Creative Work (K–2)" lesson at Common Sense Education (http://bit.ly/2nVX1bU) to support this process.

- **Mathematics:** Read the book *Perfect Square* by Michael Hall (2011). Talk about how the author used one square to create many different collages and pictures. Give each student a square and ask them to cut it and create any picture they would like by using only pieces of the square cut in any manner they like. Instruct them *not* to write their name on their paper. A few days later, hold up the designs and ask the students to identify their own work. If students struggle with this task, remind them the importance of labeling their own artwork and giving themselves credit for what they create.

Operational: Crediting the Work of Others

Learning goal:
I can locate resources that others have created and include and credit them in my projects.

As students become aware of the value of ownership, you can introduce them to the importance of crediting the work of others as they conduct research for their own work. Through self-reflection on the value of labeling one's own work, students will see the importance of crediting their peers and others with the work they create. It is also important to address the legal implications for using another person's work without properly citing the source. For K–2 students, you can keep this concept very simple by stating it is against the law to claim another person's work as your own. Additionally, through these discussions, students will begin to see great value in listening and sharing ideas from peers in order to further benefit their own growth in all areas of the learning curriculum. In this lesson, you will review resources students use to obtain information for a project. The class will collect information, and you will create a list of the sources they use to gather information on a specific topic.

Process: Researching and Crediting a Source

Use the following five steps to teach students how to locate a resource, use it to support their project, and credit that resource.

1. Introduce students to a new project. Using the chapter 4 lessons as a guide, help students search for resources applicable to that project.

2. As a group, review resources that students found.

3. Write down the information the students identified. This could involve something as simple as writing quotes on a note card or digitally through a word-processing or note-taking document.

4. Have students verbalize where they got their information. You can have them do this as a class, or you can organize them into groups where they discuss their sources with each other.

5. Have students verbalize their understanding that sources are not their own unless they have personally created them.

Connections

You can apply this lesson to different content areas in the following ways.

- **English language arts:** Have students conduct a biography research project about their favorite author. Model for students how to collect data and cite sources where they find information about the author they selected. Then, have students write down facts about the author's life and verbally cite the source where they got the information.

- **Science:** As a class, sit down and begin to investigate a science topic, such as animal research. Have students offer suggestions on sources the class can use to locate information on the new topic. With students, explore sources such as Symbaloo (www.symbaloo.com), YouTube Kids (https://kids .youtube.com), National Geographic (www.national geographic.com), and books on Epic! (www.getepic .com). Make a list of the information that you find and what sources you find it on, and then release students to meet in smaller groups or pairs to try to access some of the same research you found as a group. Have your students write down information

TECH TIP

Symbaloo (www.symbaloo .com) allows you to add numerous pages to a virtual pinboard. For example, if your class researches lions, you can add websites about lions to your Symbaloo pinboard for students to easily access. Students simply go to your Symbaloo page, click on an image, and learn from the website they access.

they find and where they find it. Students can then refer to these sources when completing their own future investigations.

Wow: Citing Resources in Digital Projects

Students who understand the value of ownership and of crediting the work of others can take the next step by learning to cite sources they use in their projects. For grades K–2 students, writing ability differs and some students may lack the motor and letter-recognition skills to type out their citations. Therefore, this lesson has them use voice notes so they can cite their sources out loud and record them for you to hear. This helps to build awareness at all development levels that citing sources is a critical step when creating digital projects.

Process: Citing a Resource

Use the following four steps to have students record a voice citation for a resource they use.

1. Prompt students to begin independent investigations on a new or known topic.

2. Have students search for, download, and save pictures that will enhance their project on the chosen topic. Some students may need prompts or support from you to properly detail the name of the website they used to obtain their information. They could also take a screenshot of the website at which they find their pictures. If they are comfortable doing so, students should create a folder in their classroom LMS space to store these images.

3. Students should take the pictures from their photo folder and insert them into their project.

4. Instruct students to record a voice note, saying the websites where they got the pictures and, if possible, each picture's photographer or illustrator.

Connections

You can apply this lesson to different content areas in the following ways.

Learning goal:

I can cite the sources that I use in my digital projects.

TEACHING TIP

By listening to student audio and checking proper source citing, as well as assessing students' knowledge about the learning target, you can assess many content areas at once.

DISCUSSION QUESTIONS

Consider the following questions for personal reflection or in collaborative work with colleagues.

▸ After reading this chapter, in what ways do you have a better understanding of the importance of teaching Internet safety?

▸ Why is it important to make the connection between physical safety and online safety lessons for young students?

continued ▸

- **English language arts:** Have students open the ChatterPix Kids (http://bit.ly/2u4arGv) application on their device and then take a picture of an illustration from a storybook they are reading. Students should record a voice note citing the book that they used for their ChatterPix Kids recording. For example, a student can record herself saying, "This is the caterpillar from the book *The Very Hungry Caterpillar* by Eric Carle." If students use an online resource, they can verbalize where they found any information or pictures online, such as by saying, "I found these penguin pictures on World Book Online."

- **Mathematics:** Ask students who work on explaining mathematics processes to record themselves saying where they found support for how they completed a process. For example, they can say, "I learned on Khan Academy that if you put two cookies and two cookies together, it makes four cookies." Students may use any LMS to upload a voice note explaining their thinking.

Conclusion

In this chapter, you introduced students to sound digital citizenship practices that will help them protect themselves and their personal information from online strangers and bullies. You also engaged students in understanding the value of ownership—of both what they create and the work that others create. In chapter 7, you will introduce students to the value of computational thinking by teaching them about the basic coding concepts that drive the digital world.

▸ Why do you need to make the connection between real-life and online strangers for students? What correlation do they have? Why is the correlation important at this age?

▸ Why do students need to know what bullying means before you discuss cyberbullying? What correlation do they have?

▸ How can you assess if students understand how a bully behaves or what a bully does?

▸ How does teaching students to write their name on their work relate to their understanding of the value of ownership?

▸ How or when would you foster a conversation with your students regarding legal implications for properly citing sources?

▸ How is citing technology resources the same as citing books or other print resources? How is it different?

▸ Because students can look up anything online, why is teaching them to recognize sources important?

▸ What online experiment could you carry out to show students how easily they can share information through social media? Share your ideas on Twitter with the hashtag #NOWClassrooms.

Expanding Technology and Coding Concepts

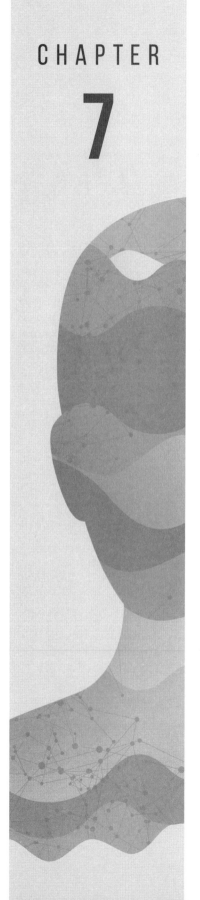

This book has discussed various procedural activities for you to try while implementing technology in your classroom. Students can continue to grow in collaboration and learning through coding and web development. Teaching students the method behind code, such as *if-then* statements, gives them an understanding of computational thinking, which is the method of organizing instructions that determines how digital devices operate. Applying this skill in the form of computer code also emphasizes the values of innovative design. You can help students understand how these concepts converge by explaining to them that designers build all their favorite digital games using coding concepts and practices. Similar to chapter 5, these are skills that also align with the ISTE (2016) standards of *computational thinker* and *innovative designer*.

Although coding may seem like an advanced topic for grades K–2 students, in *Technology and Digital Media in the Early Years*, editor Chip Donohue (2015) investigates the expansion and use of technology that is developmentally appropriate for young learners. He writes, "Research suggests that children engaging with programming are given opportunities to explore spatial concepts, problem solving, measurement, and geometry and engage with metacognitive processes" (Donohue, 2015, p. 151). Together with the four Cs (communication, collaboration, critical thinking, and creativity), programming and coding can create a tangible experience for K–2 students to understand the processes behind developing digital products.

As jobs continue to change in the 21st century, computer coding and computational thinking will be necessary in many careers throughout the world (Cook, 2014). Our current students will no longer be only consumers of technology but creators of it. In this chapter, we provide lessons you can use to help young minds understand the importance and processes of using code to create innovative designs. At the end of this chapter, students will understand the importance of coding and know how to write basic code.

Coding for Everyone

Teaching K–2 students about coding's benefits and importance helps them understand from an early age the computational thinking behind coding language, and it allows them to think outside the box when designing code to implement ideas. It also benefits students collaborating together and engaging their problem-solving skills to overcome challenges. When playing online and unplugged coding games, students often get stuck. They quickly realize when a peer has made it to a higher coding level than they have and will seek out that tech-spert to help them properly solve problems, allowing both students to advance to higher coding levels.

Coding is a universal language and not necessarily academic specific. For these lessons, we have created universal processes that relate directly to coding but that you can apply to multiple subject areas when designing lesson plans. We believe students need to learn coding concepts as part of the regular curriculum.

Novice: Understanding Basic Coding

For many teachers, the idea of learning to code sounds intimidating, but you can still help make learning to code fun and engaging for students. This lesson involves selecting coding

Learning goal:
I can understand basic coding concepts.

apps or web-based services for students to access and explore. For K–2 students, the best coding apps make a game out of the learning process. You have plenty to choose from, such as LightBot (https://lightbot.com), ScratchJr (www.scratchjr .org), Puzzlets (www.digitaldreamlabs.com/puzzlets), and Daisy the Dinosaur (www.daisythedinosaur.com), or you can make use of the resources on Code.org (https://code.org).

Exploring with games is a high-interest, motivating way for students to explore code without becoming easily frustrated. To students, an entertainment-themed coding activity is simply a game to play for fun. Beyond this initial exploration, you should be prepared to conduct a class discussion about games. Discussions can focus on the purpose of coding and how it creates directions to tell digital things what to do. Class discussions can lead to group collaboration and problem-solving skills through sharing personal examples, challenges, and how students overcame obstacles. It also allows you to analyze students who have strengths in coding and could be a tech-spert for certain games or other tasks that require strong computational-thinking skills.

Process: Playing Basic Coding Games

Use the following four steps to introduce students to basic coding apps or websites.

1. Select the apps or websites you want students to use to learn about coding. Try out some of the apps or websites we list in this section that allow students to play coding games and become familiar with them before teaching students.

2. Have students explore the apps or websites you selected without any initial instruction. As they explore, begin to help them problem solve and conduct an open conversation about their goals relative to the app or website features they are looking at. Specific goals are unique to each game which is why teacher preview is important. For example, in LightBot, users code a robot to light up boxes. Code.org users pick the challenge and goals they want to accomplish.

3. Have students put their devices away and sit with you as a group to discuss what they had to do in the coding games that they played.

4. Talk with your students about the purpose behind those games. For example, they might say, "We had to get the alien to light up all the boxes to complete the level." Explain that this is what coding is—creating directions that tell devices what to do.

Connections

You can apply this lesson to different content areas in the following ways.

- **English language arts:** Set up a classroom learning center where students can explore a few coding games during free-exploration time. This learning center's purpose is to activate prior knowledge about coding and help students develop their vocabulary on the topic. You can have students work independently or with a partner. In either case, allowing them free discovery of coding games fosters their interest and engagement in beginning coding.

- **Social science:** Use the illustration titled the Techie Timeline at Tes Teach (http://bit.ly/2tGWm1O) to lead a class discussion about the history of computing. At home working with a parent, have students create a timeline of technology tools they have used in their life outside of school, creating a similar historic visual that is personal to them.

Operational: Coding While Unplugged

Learning goal:
I can code something or someone using computational thinking.

Coding skills go beyond the computer and into computational thinking for our students. We want students to be able to use computational thinking to understand cause and effect, meaning, "If I do A, then B will happen." To teach students what coding truly is—a precise set of simple instructions—use this lesson to teach students *unplugged coding*. Have them give explicit directions for a student or you to get from one end of the classroom to the other. This hands-on lesson helps students understand the importance of conversation, collaboration, creative thinking, and precision. It also helps them begin to understand how coding languages operate and why they work.

Process: Coding the Teacher

Use the following seven steps to teach students how to give simple unplugged coding instructions.

1. Lay out a path in the classroom for you, the teacher, to walk. For example, put painter's tape on the floor from your desk to the door. Students must learn how to *code the teacher* by providing very precise instructions to tell you how to get from point A to point B.

2. Stand at point A, and tell students that they must get you to point B.

3. Have students determine the direction you should walk by saying things such as, "Walk forward."

4. When one student says this, simply walk forward without stopping. This may lead to you bumping into items or walls in the classroom. This teaches students that they need to give more than this one direction.

5. Be sure students tell you to, for example, "walk forward one step" or "turn right" for each pace. Let them collaborate and figure this out, only hinting at what they need to do.

6. Instruct students to talk about what directions they need to give you to get you to point B. This allows them to discover that they need to provide very specific directions. For example, you cannot sit in a chair until students specifically say to sit down.

7. Upon completion, reflect with students on how they engaged in collaboration and critical thinking to guide you to your destination. Emphasize the parallels between the simple instructions they needed to provide to you and how coding languages work to instruct digital devices.

Connections

You can apply this lesson to different content areas in the following ways.

- **English language arts:** Have students work with a partner or small group to mimic this section's lesson process by coding one group member from one place in the classroom to another. Students can record their steps with pencil and paper using words or symbols and exchange directions with another group to try to see if the code they wrote was successful. When complete, facilitate a class discussion on how they used group-collaboration and problem-solving skills throughout the unplugged coding experience.

- **Science:** Have partners practice sequencing numbers as they discuss how important it is to use transitional words like *first*, *second*, and *next*. Each group should create a sequence of numbers in a digital document and share that with you through the classroom LMS.

Wow: Coding a Simple Toy

When students better understand the concept of coding, you can introduce small-group, hands-on work with coding toys. Working together to code a simple toy teaches them about coding in a fun and age-appropriate way. This lesson uses classroom coding toys, such as Bee-Bot (www.bee-bot.us), Ozobot (http://ozobot.com), Sphero (www.sphero.com), or Puzzlets (www.digitaldreamlabs.com) to enhance learning how to code with play. Using hands-on, programmable toys will help students better understand coding structure and how each step in the process builds on previous steps.

Process: Programming a Toy

Use the following ten steps to teach students how to program a classroom coding toy. (This process focuses on Bee-Bot, but you can adapt it to other programmable toys.)

1. In short independent learning center rotations, have students explore the coding toy you provide to them. Allow students time to collaboratively discover and play with the toy.

2. Formally introduce the toy to students.

3. Explain to students that the toy will not move unless given directions via code.

Learning goal:
I can use a coding toy to understand how basic coding works.

TEACHING TIP

Most coding toys come at an expense; however, some coding toy companies have demo programs. You may try contacting the makers of coding toys to see if they give any demo coding toys to educators. Schools can also partner with a local library or the state to receive grants to use toward purchasing tech toys for classroom use.

4. Discuss the symbols and the meaning of the symbols the toy understands and the directions that it needs to receive for it to move.

5. Put paper arrows down on the ground, and have students verbally tell you the correct buttons to push to move the toy in the directions the arrows indicate.

6. Place the toy on the ground, and ask students which direction it should move. (The Bee-Bot includes options for special mats and grids it can navigate that you might find particularly useful.)

7. Have students give you directions for the toy.

8. Program the toy to behave as the students direct. With a Bee-Bot, for example, if students instruct it to move forward, push the forward button the amount of times they have specified, and allow students to see it move.

9. Problem solve with students to make the toy move about the room or, with Bee-Bot, navigate the mat or grid. Make sure you model failure by showing students what happens if you don't correctly program the toy.

10. Model how to start over from the beginning and different ways in which students can plan their directions. You can then give them opportunities to use the toy in small groups.

Connections

You can apply this lesson to different content areas in the following ways.

- **English language arts:** Create a Bee-Bot mat that is related to a current learning target. For example, you might create a mat that has alphabet letters in a random pattern. Have students work in small groups to use coding instructions to move a Bee-Bot successfully through the correct sequence. (You can adapt this connection to robot toys other than Bee-Bot.)

DISCUSSION QUESTIONS

Consider the following questions for personal reflection or in collaborative work with colleagues.

▸ What did you understand about computer coding before this chapter? What do you know now?

▸ How has the world evolved to create such a heavy push to understand computer coding?

▸ Why must elementary students progress from playing online games to using unplugged coding to using coding apps to coding physical devices?

▸ How do coding activities teach students collaboration and teamwork?

▸ Why or how would you encourage students to collaboratively work and problem solve to create and solve simple coding assignments?

▸ Can you think of professionals who work in coding or with computers you could invite to come in and share their knowledge with your students? How could this have meaning for students?

continued ▸

▸ How does teaching a student basic coding have a direct impact on our world and the student's possible future career?

▸ How can coding allow for enhanced problem-solving and critical-thinking skills? How could coding have other benefits in the classroom?

▸ How can you connect coding with student storytelling and creative thinking?

▸ Does your own knowledge (or lack of knowledge) of coding make you feel comfortable or uncomfortable with teaching beginning coding skills? Why is this the case?

- **Mathematics:** Have groups of students do some online shopping (without actual purchases) to locate the different types of coding toys that are on the market. Instruct each group to create a table in a digital document to compare products and pricing. Each group should partner with another group to compare the toys they found and discuss which toys look most interesting relative to their cost. Once complete, the groups should submit their charts using the classroom LMS.

Conclusion

In this chapter, you introduced students to how they can use computational-thinking and innovative-design skills to learn the basics of computer coding. Congratulations on reaching the last of this book's lessons! In the epilogue, we offer some reflection on educating K–2 students in a digital world.

Epilogue:
Looking Forward

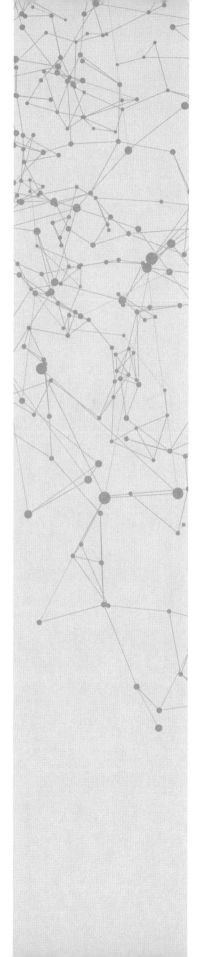

On a school walkthrough in May of 2016, in the role of an instructional coach, Meg observed a librarian teaching a lesson to high school sophomores. The lesson covered how students could create a digital movie, but it lacked any focus on meaningful curriculum connections. The librarian's lesson used a teacher-directed rubric to properly cover the basics of how to create a digital movie. The final projects all looked very similar, with little variance or creativity, because most of these students had no previous experience in digital moviemaking.

Contrast this with a kindergarten class Meg visited the week before. The five- and six-year-old students independently snapped digital pictures, located the images in a photo album app, and used them to create movie trailers. Groups collaborated as they planned and created movie trailers complete with animations, transitions, credits, and soundtracks. Each student could tell us the learning outcome and purpose of the assignment. When the groups completed their task, each student independently saved the project to a personal digital portfolio. The students could not wait to share their movie trailers with the rest of the class, their parents, and the world via their teacher's Twitter account.

Wow, talk about the need to close the gap! The five- and six-year-old students independently created their work and shared it with the world. The high school sophomores, about ten years older and only two years from college or career, were only just creating their first movie. The high schoolers worked alone and checked off checkboxes on a rubric (which resulted in very similar final projects), while the elementary students went wild with their creativity.

Which class would you rather teach? Which class would your students rather learn in?

The labels *college ready* and *career ready* seem slightly out of place in a kindergarten classroom, but these beginning elementary students develop a technology foundation that will make them successful in the future no matter what tools, apps, or websites they encounter. Change will remain the constant part of their digital future, and these young learners have a safe head start with online safety, avoidance of cyberbullying, and the basics of becoming a digital citizen.

More important than learning how to use the technology tools and apps, these students start to develop the four Cs of communication, collaboration, critical thinking, and creativity. Repeatedly, employers such as Sevenshift CEO Caroline Webb (2016) report that young adults need these super skills when they enter the workforce. You may find it hard to think of young learners juxtaposed with high school and college students, but now is when we develop the foundation for their future successes. As educators, we need to create learning opportunities that focus on content and the four Cs for learners of all ages. We make it our collaborative mission to create flexible, creative lifelong learners. Learners should find learning fun and collaborative at all ages!

Although we have confidence that you now have fostered the foundational skills your K–2 students need to succeed throughout their educational career, our team has many more ideas that we could not fit into this book. As we plan our next writing project, we will share ideas, photos, and student work on Twitter with the #NOWClassrooms hashtag. Let your own learning continue there and on our blog. Our group plans to continue to work and write together well into the future because our personal professional development network has become so important to each of us. Check our blog for upcoming conference dates where *NOW Classrooms* authors will be presenting as well as for additional resources and frequently updated lesson ideas.

The sharing continues as we invite you into our classrooms to see learning in action. We include information about booking us for professional development in this book's About the Authors section. If a field trip will not work for your team, we can virtually open our classrooms to you using technology tools like Skype and Google Hangouts. We will happily share our students' work while answering any questions you might have.

Students are the focus of our work, and along the journey of this book, students have explored and created projects that they could not have created prior to the evolution of smartphones, tablets, and apps. These projects have made young learners ready for the ever-changing digital landscape of the future. From novice to operational to wow, you have promoted the foundational NOW skills to prepare students for the challenges and changes ahead.

Appendix: Glossary of Tools and Terms

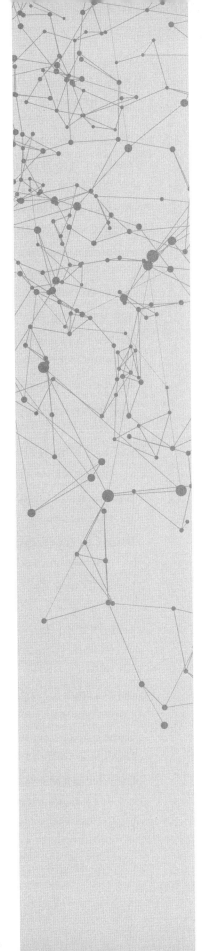

This appendix includes a list of terms and resources we introduced and used throughout the book. Apps, programs, and websites are listed, as well as digital and academic terms that will aid you in lesson planning both NOW and in the future.

1:1 or one to one: Describes the number of technology devices (iPads, laptops, Chromebooks) given to each student in an academic setting; a 1:1 school has one device per each student

1:2 or one to two: Describes the number of technology devices (iPads, laptops, Chromebooks) given to each student in an academic setting; a 2:1 school means that one technology device is available for every two students in an academic setting. Two classes may share one class set, or students may partner up to use devices.

10 Frame Fill (www.classroomfocusedsoftware .com/10framefill.html): A mathematics app that uses the ten-frame concept with drag-and-drop manipulatives

ABCya (www.abcya.com): An educational app with games for students pre-K through fifth grade

ABC Magnetic Alphabet (https://itunes.apple.com/us/app/abc-magnetic -alphabet-lite-for-kids/id389132393?mt=8): An app reminiscent of a chalkboard that uses virtual magnetic letters that students can manipulate into any configuration

anchor chart: A chart for making thinking visible during the learning process while recording strategies, processes, guidelines, and other content

Animals A–Z (http://a-z-animals.com): An online encyclopedia with information about a huge variety of animals

Animoto (https://animoto.com): A video creation website and app with limited free features and options for educator accounts (see https://animoto.com/education /classroom)

app smashing: The process of using multiple apps to create projects or complete tasks

ArtStudio (www.luckyclan.com): An app that includes a sketching, drawing, and photo editing tool

Bee-Bot (www.bee-bot.us): An introductory coding toy for elementary students

Big Brown Bear keyboarding (www.bigbrownbear.co.uk/keyboard): A simple website for learning beginning keyboarding skills

Blabberize (http://blabberize.com): A website that mixes together an uploaded picture and recorded speech to make it seem like the picture is talking

Blackboard (www.blackboard.com): An educational technology services company that includes comprehensive LMS products

Book Creator (https://bookcreator.com): An app students can use to create, share, and publish their own ebooks

BookFlix (www.scholastic.com/digital/bookflix.htm): A digital resource that pairs fictional video stories with nonfiction ebooks

BrainPOP Jr. (https://jr.brainpop.com): A website that features short, animated educational videos for students in grades K–3 that also includes quizzes and related materials

camera app: The app found on most portable devices that gives access to its camera for taking photos or recording video

Canvas (www.canvaslms.com/k-12): An LMS software tool for organizing students' digital work and managing, tracking, and reporting educational data and courses

ChatterPix Kids (www.duckduckmoose.com/educational-iphone-itouch-apps -for-kids/chatterpixkids): An iPad- and iPhone-only app that students can use to record their voice, select a picture to attach the recording to, and play the recording back as if the object says what the students recorded

Chirbit (www.chirbit.com): An app and website that allow users to record voice memos and export voice memos as QR codes or as social media posts

cloud computing: The practice of using a network of remote, Internet-hosted servers to store, manage, and process data

Code.org (https://code.org): A website for learning coding and programming on iPads, Chromebooks, and Android devices

Common Sense (www.commonsense.org): A collection of articles, videos, and resources to use for teaching digital citizenship; connects with offshoots Common Sense Media (www.commonsensemedia.org) and Common Sense Education (www.commonsense.org/education)

D2L (www.d2l.com): A technology-based learning company that offers a comprehensive K–12-focused LMS platform

Daisy the Dinosaur (www.daisythedinosaur.com): An introductory coding app

Dropbox (www.dropbox.com): A free, cloud-based service for storing and sharing files

Edge (www.microsoft.com/en-us/windows/microsoft-edge): A Microsoft-developed web browser that has replaced Microsoft Internet Explorer

Edmodo (www.edmodo.com): A global education network that allows students to collaborate and access resources

Educreations (www.educreations.com): An interactive screencast whiteboard with free and premium options that students can use to record their learning

Epic! (www.getepic.com): A website and app that provide students with a digital library of high-interest books

Explain Everything (https://explaineverything.com): A paid collaborative and interactive whiteboard website and app for Android and Apple devices as well as a Google Chrome extension

FaceTime (https://itunes.apple.com/us/app/facetime/id414307850?mt=12): A video telephone and video chat service for conducting one-on-one video calls among Apple devices

Flickr (www.flickr.com): A free website for searching for images that includes Explore functions and a Creative Commons category with images in the public domain

Flipagram (https://flipagram.com): An app that allows users to create short video stories with photos, video, and music

flipped learning: A learning model where the traditional classroom work–homework model is flipped—students watch video lectures at home and work on exercises, projects, and discussions in class

G Suite for Education (www.google.com/intl/en_us/edu/): An overarching term for all the Google products that a school system has available for staff and student use

glitch: A problem that arises when using technology

Global Read Aloud (https://theglobalreadaloud.com): A reading program that connects classrooms through common read alouds

Gmail (https://mail.google.com): Google's email platform

Google (www.google.com): A search engine developed by Google

Google Chrome (www.google.com/chrome): A Google-developed web browser that you can use on any device and that has additional features such as extensions and the ability to sync bookmarks across all devices

Google Chrome Web Store (https://chrome.google.com/webstore/category/apps): A place to discover apps, games, extensions, and themes for Google Chrome

Google Classroom (https://classroom.google.com): A file management system with some features of an LMS that allows classrooms to share announcements and documents and conduct discussions

Google Docs (www.google.com/docs/about): A G Suite for Education word processing tool for creating and editing documents independently or in collaborative groups available to all teachers and students who are members of the Google domain through their school

Google Drawings (https://drawings.google.com): A drawing app within G Suite for Education

Google Drive (www.google.com/drive): A cloud-based storage platform that can store and sync files across multiple devices using a single login

Google Earth (www.google.com/earth): An interactive satellite map of the world

Google Hangouts (https://hangouts.google.com): A unified communications service that allows members to initiate and participate in text, voice, and video chats either one-on-one or in a group and that is built into Google+ and Gmail and available as an app for Apple and Android devices

Google Keep (https://keep.google.com): A cloud-based tool for gathering and organizing notes, lists, and ideas and sharing them for online collaboration

Google Maps (https://maps.google.com): A Google tool that students can use to generate maps to support their learning

Google Photos (https://photos.google.com): A photo storage, organization, and editing website, formerly called Picasa

Google Sheets (www.google.com/sheets/about): A G Suite for Education spreadsheet program that supports common spreadsheet functions such as data entry, sorting, number calculation, and chart creation

Google Slides (www.google.com/slides/about): A web-based presentation creator in G Suite for Education that allows users to insert images, text, charts, and videos, as well as modify transitions, layouts, and backgrounds

Google+ (https://plus.google.com): A social network where users can connect over a variety of interests; many educators post ideas, questions, and requests to connect with other classrooms through Skype, Google Hangouts, and blogging

Hour of Code (https://code.org/learn): An international event to encourage students of all ages to try coding; schools, public libraries, and community organizations hold programs where participants can try their hand at website building, game creation, graphic design, and more

i-nigma (www.i-nigma.com/i-nigmahp.html): A QR code scanner website

iMovie (www.apple.com/imovie): An Apple iOS and MacOS video-editing tool for creating high-quality movies; users can import photos, videos, music, and sound effects and use filters and special effects to enhance movie content

Instagram (www.instagram.com): An online photo- and video-sharing social networking site

interactive whiteboard: An interactive classroom display board, often referred to as a *SMART Board* even though many different manufacturers exist, including SMART Technologies, Promethean, and Mimio

Internet Live Stats (www.internetlivestats.com): A site for monitoring how many users are using the Internet

iWriteWords (https://itunes.apple.com/us/app/iwritewords-handwriting-game /id307025309?mt=8): A simple letter-tracing app

Kahoot! (https://getkahoot.com): A free website for creating quizzes and answering the questions from any digital device

Keynote (www.apple.com/keynote): The Apple presentation tool for iOS and MacOS devices

Khan Academy (www.khanacademy.org): A screencast tutorial website for students to watch videos and check their understanding of concepts

Kidblog (https://kidblog.org): A website where students can publish and share their learning in a secure environment

KidRex (www.kidrex.org): A student-friendly search engine for researching content

KWL: A type of graphic organizer designed to help students learn by asking them the following questions: What do we know about this already? What do we wonder about this? What did we learn about this?

learning goal: An expectation and target for what students should learn and know

learning management system (LMS): Software used to manage, track, and report educational data and courses

LightBot (https://lightbot.com): An introductory coding website and app

Microsoft Excel (https://products.office.com/en-us/excel): A spreadsheet program that you can use on both Apple and Windows devices that makes up part of the Microsoft Office suite

Microsoft Office (https://products.office.com): A productivity-oriented software suite that contains Word, PowerPoint, Excel, and other Microsoft programs

Microsoft PowerPoint (https://products.office.com/en-us/powerpoint): A presentation creation tool in Microsoft Office used to create slideshows incorporating images, text, video, and audio

Microsoft Word (https://products.office.com/en-us/word): A word processing app that is part of the Microsoft Office suite

Moodle (httsp://moodle.org): An online learning platform for creating personalized learning environments

Mozilla Firefox (www.mozilla.org/en-US/firefox/new): A web browser

My Storybook (www.mystorybook.com): A simple book creation website

Mystery Skype (https://education.microsoft.com/skype-in-the-classroom /mystery-skype): A service offered on the Skype website to help teachers connect and collaborate with another unknown classroom

National Geographic (www.nationalgeographic.com): Houses a collection of information about geography, cartography, and exploration

National Geographic Kids (http://kids.nationalgeographic.com): A kid-friendly version of National Geographic with a collection of information and games

Newsela (https://newsela.com): A site with leveled news, primary sources, standards-aligned formative assessments, and more that includes free content and premium features

Notes: A default iOS app that allows users to take and share notes

The NOW Classrooms Project (http://nowclassrooms.com): A website about the entire NOW Classrooms Project, including the *NOW Classrooms* blog and details about the book series

Otus (http://otus.com): A classroom LMS that integrates data from third parties to get a more comprehensive snapshot about student growth

Ozobot (www.ozobot.com): Small coding robots that help teach students how to code

Padlet (https://padlet.com): A digital bulletin board for student collaborative projects that students join through a code the teacher provides

PebbleGo (www.pebblego.com): A series of databases for beginning researchers enriched with audio and video media

PicCollage (https://pic-collage.com): A free media mashup app (with in-app purchases) for all devices that allows students to add pictures, stickers, and backgrounds and use various templates

PicMonkey (www.picmonkey.com): A free online image editor

Pinterest (www.pinterest.com): A digital, visual bulletin board with ideas and links to a variety of teaching and learning ideas

PowerSchool Learning (www.powerschoolcom/solutions/lms): An LMS from PowerSchool for K–12 school systems

Puzzlets (www.digitaldreamlabs.com): A coding game by Digital Dream Labs that uses a puzzle board and puzzle pieces to help students learn how to code

QR code: A scannable code that links to online information

QR Reader (https://itunes.apple.com/us/app/qr-reader-for-iphone/id368494609 ?mt=8): A free QR code reader for the iPhone

QuickVoice (www.nfinityinc.com/quickvoiceip.html): A voice recorder for iOS devices

Raz-Kids (www.raz-kids.com): A digital guided-reading program that provides teachers with digital, downloadable, and printable books

Remind (www.remind.com): A website that allows users to send messages to other users' devices

Reminders: A default iOS app that allows users to make a list of reminders

Safari (www.apple.com/safari): An Apple-developed web browser that can only be used on iOS and MacOS devices

Safe Search Kids (www.safesearchkids.com): A search engine for students

Scan (www.scan.me): A QR code reader

Scholastic Story Starters (www.scholastic.com/teachers/story-starters): A website where teachers can have students build stories

Schoolkit Math (www.schoolkitapps.com): An app that provides virtual mathematics manipulatives

Schoology (www.schoology.com): A learning management system containing a discussion board where students can write posts in response to an ongoing discussion

Scratch (https://scratch.mit.edu): A free coding language and online community developed by MIT that acts as the basis for Google CS First courses and tutorials

ScratchJr (https://itunes.apple.com/us/app/scratchjr/id895485086?mt=8): A tool for learning a programming language

screencast: A recording of a digital screen with audio added to explain a concept

Screencastify (www.screencastify.com): An extension of the Chrome browser, or an application that users can install and run through the Chrome browser; it is a screen recorder that can capture video or screenshots

screenshot: An image of the display on a computer screen

Seesaw (http://web.seesaw.me): A site and app for creating student-driven digital portfolios, with free basic features, premium advanced features, and school versions

Shadow Puppet Edu (http://get-puppet.co): An app that allows students to make simple video slide shows

Showbie (www.showbie.com): A learning management system used to give and receive assignments while allowing for feedback

Skype (www.skype.com): An Internet-based communications app that facilitates audio and video communication among multiple parties

Skype in the Classroom (https://education.microsoft.com/skype-in-the -classroom/overview): An online community where teachers can find resources to use Skype in their classrooms, including information on guest speakers, Mystery Skype, virtual field trips, and lesson plans

Sphero (www.sphero.com): A robotic toy that users can code using a corresponding app

Stickies (www.zhornsoftware.co.uk/stickies): A website that provides a downloadable program for using digital sticky notes on a PC

Sticky (www.stickynotesapp.com): An iOS app that mimics sticky notes on the screen

Symbaloo (www.symbaloo.com): A social bookmarking website to organize research tools for students to access that works similarly to a hyperdoc but has much more visual appeal

Tangram Free (https://itunes.apple.com/us/app/tangram-free /id400629406?mt=8): A mathematics app that uses tangram shapes

tech-spert: An expert in a certain technology task, website, or application

Trello (https://trello.com): A free website and app that allow students to create and organize lists within online boards; users can share Trello boards with each other, making task assignment and voting easy for group projects

Twitter (https://twitter.com): A social networking service that enables users to send short messages (or *tweets*) to their followers

Twitter Analytics (https://analytics.twitter.com): A Twitter tool for reviewing and analyzing activity on a Twitter account

TypingClub (www.typingclub.com): A website that teaches typing

unplugged coding: An activity one can conduct without the use of a computer or electronic equipment to understand how computer coding works

Voice Memos: An iOS app that allows you to record audio, edit your recorded audio, and export the file

WeVideo (www.wevideo.com): A video creation and video-sharing tool that uses cloud-based video-editing software and includes free and premium features

World Book Online (http://worldbookonline.com): An online encyclopedia, dictionary, and atlas

Writing Wizard (http://lescapadou.com): A tablet app that allows students to trace and learn letters, sight words, and teacher-created word lists; it is accessible through iTunes or the Google Play Store

YouTube (www.youtube.com): A video platform for publishing and viewing video content

YouTube Kids (https://kids.youtube.com): A student-friendly video-sharing app for finding and viewing student-safe videos

References and Resources

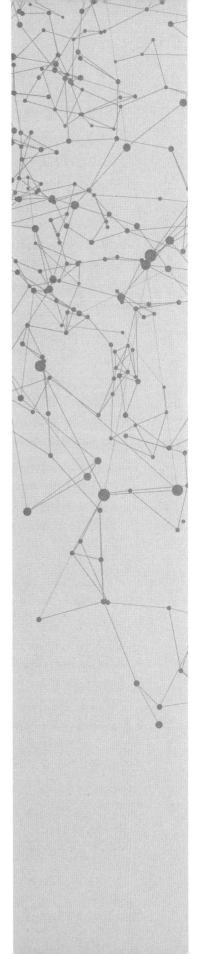

Allen, R. (2017, February 6). *What happens online in 60 seconds?* Accessed at www.smartinsights.com/internet -marketing-statistics/happens-online-60-seconds on July 27, 2017.

Azzam, A. M. (2014). Motivated to learn: A conversation with Daniel Pink. *Educational Leadership, 72*(1), 12–17.

Belgrad, S., Burke, K., & Fogarty, R. (2008). *The portfolio connection: Student work linked to standards* (3rd ed.). Thousand Oaks, CA: Corwin Press.

Bellanca, J., & Brandt, R. (Eds.). (2010). *21st century skills: Rethinking how students learn.* Bloomington, IN: Solution Tree Press.

Bergmann, J., & Sams, A. (2014). *Flipped learning: Gateway to student engagement.* Eugene, OR: International Society for Technology in Education.

Bitner, N., & Bitner, J. (2002). Integrating technology into the classroom: Eight keys to success. *Journal of Technology and Teacher Education, 10*(1), 95–100.

Block, J. (2014, October 30). *Student choice leads to student voice* [Blog post]. Accessed at www.edutopia.org/blog /student-choice-leads-to-voice-joshua-block on January 16, 2017.

Brookhart, S. M. (2008). *Types of feedback and their purposes.* Accessed at www.ascd.org/publications/books/108019/chapters/Types-of-Feedback-and-Their-Purposes.aspx on February 10, 2014.

Chappuis, J. (2012). "How am I doing?" *Educational Leadership, 70*(1), 36–41.

Children's Online Privacy Protection Act of 1998, 15 U.S.C. §§ 6501–6505.

Clowes, G. (2011). *The essential 5: A starting point for Kagan Cooperative Learning.* Accessed at www.kaganonline.com/free_articles/research_and_rationale/330/The-Essential-5-A-Starting-Point-for-Kagan-Cooperative-Learning on July 18, 2017.

Common Sense Media. (2014). *Pause and think online* [Video file]. Accessed at www.commonsensemedia.org/videos/pause-think-online on April 10, 2017.

Cook, D. (2014, February 7). Why every child should learn to code. *The Guardian.* Accessed at www.theguardian.com/technology/2014/feb/07/year-of-code-dan-crow-songkick on July 18, 2017.

Crockett, L. W., & Churches, A. (2018). *Growing global digital citizens: Better practices that build better learners.* Bloomington, IN: Solution Tree Press.

Curran, B., & Wetherbee, N. (2014). *Engaged, connected, empowered: Teaching and learning in the 21st century.* New York: Routledge.

Donohue, C. (Ed.). (2015). *Technology and digital media in the early years: Tools for teaching and learning.* New York: Routledge.

DuFour, R., DuFour, R., Eaker, R., & Karhanek, G. (2010). *Raising the bar and closing the gap: Whatever it takes.* Bloomington, IN: Solution Tree Press.

Ferriter, W. M. (2014, November 11). *Are there WRONG ways to use technology?* [Blog post]. Accessed at www.solutiontree.com/blog/wrong-ways-to-use-technology on February 13, 2017.

Ferriter, W. M., & Garry, A. (2010). *Teaching the iGeneration: 5 easy ways to introduce essential skills with web 2.0 tools.* Bloomington, IN: Solution Tree Press.

Ferriter, W. M., Ramsden, J. T., & Sheninger, E. C. (2011). *Communicating and connecting with social media.* Bloomington, IN: Solution Tree Press.

Fullan, M., & Donnelly, K. (2013, July 16). *Alive in the swamp: Assessing digital innovations in education.* Accessed at www.nesta.org.uk/publications/alive-swamp-assessing-digital-innovations-education on February 13, 2017.

Fullan, M., & Langworthy, M. (2013, June). *Towards a new end: New pedagogies for deep learning.* Seattle, WA: Collaborative Impact.

Gordon, J. (2007). *The energy bus: 10 rules to fuel your life, work, and team with positive energy.* Hoboken, NJ: Wiley.

Graham, E. (n.d.). *Showcasing student work.* Accessed at www.nea.org/tools/57917.htm on July 25, 2017.

Gregory, G. H., & Chapman, C. (2013). *Differentiated instructional strategies: One size doesn't fit all* (3rd ed.). Thousand Oaks, CA: Corwin Press.

Gutierrez, K. (2016, June 21). *What are personal learning networks?* [Blog post]. Accessed at http://info.shiftelearning.com/blog/personal-learning-networks on April 12, 2017.

Hall, M. (2011). *Perfect square.* New York: HarperCollins Children's.

Hattie, J. (2009). *Visible learning: A synthesis of over 800 meta-analyses relating to achievement.* New York: Routledge.

Hattie, J. (2012a). Know thy impact. *Educational Leadership, 70*(1), 18–23.

Hattie, J. (2012b). *Visible learning for teachers: Maximizing impact on learning.* New York: Routledge.

International Society for Technology in Education. (2008). *ISTE standards for teachers.* Accessed at www.iste.org/standards/standards/standards-for-teachers on April 4, 2017.

International Society for Technology in Education. (2016). *ISTE standards for students.* Accessed at www.iste.org/standards/standards/for-students-2016 on April 4, 2017.

Keengwe, J., Onchwari, G., & Onchwari, J. (2009). Technology and student learning: Toward a learner-centered teaching model. *Association for the Advancement of Computing in Education Journal, 17*(1), 11–22.

National Governors Association Center for Best Practices & Council of Chief State School Officers. (2010). *Common Core State Standards for English language arts and literacy in history/social studies, science, and technical subjects.* Washington, DC: Authors. Accessed at www.corestandards.org/assets/CCSSI_ELA%20Standards.pdf on April 24, 2017.

National Research Council. (1999). *How people learn: Brain, mind, experience, and school.* Washington, DC: National Academies Press.

Ormiston, M. (2016). *Create future-ready classrooms, now!* Bloomington, IN: Solution Tree Press.

Otoshi, K. (2008). *One.* Mill Valley, CA: KO Kids Books.

Partnership for 21st Century Learning. (n.d.). *We're taking teaching and learning above and beyond* [Poster]. Accessed at www.p21.org/storage/documents/4csposter.pdf on March 8, 2017.

Partnership for 21st Century Learning. (2015). *The 4Cs research series.* Accessed at www.p21.org/our-work/4cs-research-series on March 8, 2017.

Pogrow, S. (2009). *Teaching content outrageously: How to captivate all students and accelerate learning, grades 4–12.* San Francisco: Jossey-Bass.

Puentedura, R. R. (2012, August 23). *The SAMR model: Background and exemplars.* Accessed at www.hippasus.com/rrpweblog/archives/2012/08/23/SAMR _BackgroundExemplars.pdf on March 8, 2017.

Puentedura, R. R. (2014, June 29). *Learning, technology, and the SAMR model: Goals, processes, and practice.* Accessed at www.hippasus.com/rrpweblog/archives/2014/06/29 /LearningTechnologySAMRModel.pdf on March 8, 2017.

Rainie, L., & Anderson, J. (2017, May 3). *The future of jobs and jobs training.* Accessed at www.pewinternet.org/2017/05/03/the-future-of-jobs-and-jobs-training on July 26, 2017.

Ribble, M. (2011). *Digital citizenship in schools* (2nd ed.). Eugene, OR: International Society for Technology in Education.

Schiller, S. Z. (2009). Practicing learner-centered teaching: Pedagogical design and assessment of a second life project. *Journal of Information Systems Education, 20*(3), 369–381.

Speck, M., & Knipe, C. (2001). *Why can't we get it right? Professional development in our schools.* Thousand Oaks, CA: Corwin Press.

Taranto, G., Dalbon, M., & Gaetano, J. (2011). Academic social networking brings web 2.0 technologies to the middle grades. *Middle School Journal, 42*(5), 12–19.

Tate, M. L. (2012). *"Sit and get" won't grow dendrites: 20 professional learning strategies that engage the adult brain* (2nd ed.). Thousand Oaks, CA: Corwin Press.

Tomlinson, C. A., & McTighe, J. (2006). *Integrating differentiated instruction and understanding by design: Connecting content and kids.* Alexandria, VA: Association for Supervision and Curriculum Development.

Tovani, C. (2012). Feedback is a two-way street. *Educational Leadership, 70*(1), 48–51.

Utah Education Network. (2003). *Learning centers.* Accessed at www.uen.org /k-2educator/learning_centers.shtml on April 5, 2017.

Visible Learning. (n.d.). *Hattie ranking: 195 influences and effect sizes related to student achievement.* Accessed at http://visible-learning.org/hattie-ranking-influences-effect -sizes-learning-achievement on December 3, 2013.

Wald, P. J., & Castleberry, M. S. (Eds.). (2000). *Educators as learners: Creating a professional learning community in your school.* Alexandria, VA: Association for Supervision and Curriculum Development.

Waters, J. (n.d.). *How to scan a QR code.* Accessed at www.dummies.com/business /marketing/social-media-marketing/how-to-scan-a-qr-code on May 1, 2017.

Webb, C. (2016, August 31). *7 science-backed skills that will make you better at your job.* Accessed at www.weforum.org/agenda/2016/08/skills-that-will-make-you-love-your-job on July 21, 2017.

Wiggins, G. (2012). Seven keys to effective feedback. *Educational Leadership, 70*(1), 10–16.

Willems, M. (2003). *Don't let the Pigeon drive the bus!* New York: Hyperion Books for Children.

Index

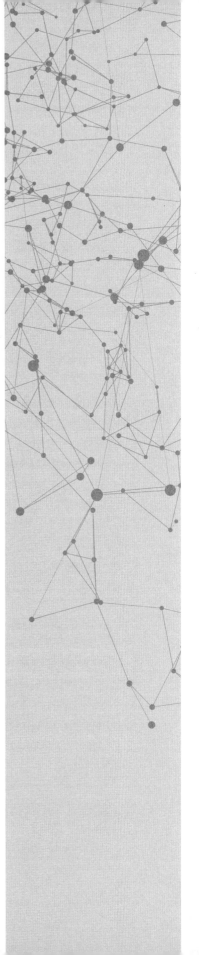

Now Classrooms Series
Meg Ormiston et al.
This practical series presents classroom-tested lessons that educators can rely on to engage students in active learning, critical thinking, and problem solving. Use these lessons to connect technology to key learning outcomes and prepare learners to succeed in the 21st century.
BKF797, BKF798, BKF799, BKF800, BKF801

Creating a Digital-Rich Classroom
Meg Ormiston
Design and deliver standards-based lessons in which technology plays an integral role. This book provides a research base and practical strategies for using web 2.0 tools to create engaging lessons that transform and enrich content.
BKF385

Designing Teacher-Student Partnership Classrooms
Meg Ormiston
Discover how teachers can become learning partners with their students. Cultivate a classroom environment in which students can apply what they've learned, teach it to their teacher and fellow students, and understand how their knowledge will be useful beyond the classroom.
BKF680

Create Future-Ready Classrooms, Now!
Meg Ormiston
Unite pedagogy and technology to inspire systemic school change. Explore digital tools that help seamlessly incorporate the technology-rich world into the classroom, understand how to use media for deeper learning, and examine a new approach to engagement and recognition.
BKF633

Solution Tree | Press

a division of
Solution Tree

Visit solution-tree.com or call 800.733.6786 to order.

Wait! Your professional development journey doesn't have to end with the last pages of this book.

We realize improving student learning doesn't happen overnight. And your school or district shouldn't be left to puzzle out all the details of this process alone.

No matter where you are on the journey, we're committed to helping you get to the next stage.

Take advantage of everything from **custom workshops** to **keynote presentations** and **interactive web and video conferencing**. We can even help you develop an action plan tailored to fit your specific needs.

Let's get the conversation started.

Call 888.763.9045 today.

SolutionTree.com